Project AIR FORCE | RAND

NATO and Caspian Security

A Mission Too Far?

Richard Sokolsky · Tanya Charlick-Paley

Prepared for the United States Air Force

The research described in this report was sponsored by the United States Air Force under Contract F49642-96-C-0001. Further information may be obtained from the Strategic Planning Division, Directorate of Plans, Hq USAF.

Library of Congress Cataloging-in-Publication Data

Sokolsky, Richard. .
    NATO and Caspian security : a mission too far? / Richard
Sokolsky and Tanya Charlick-Paley.
      p.   cm.
    "Prepared for the United States Air Force by RAND's Project
AIR FORCE. "
    "MR-1074-AF."
    Includes bibliographical references (p.).
    ISBN 0-8330-2750-6
    1. National security—Caspian Sea Region. 2. Caspian Sea
Region—Defenses. 3. North Atlantic Treaty Organization.
I. Charlick-Paley, Tanya, 1968-   II. Title. III. RAND.
UA853.C27S65   1999
355 ' .0330475—dc21   99-31661
                                                 CIP

Published 1999 by RAND
1700 Main Street, P.O. Box 2138, Santa Monica, CA 90407-2138
1333 H St., N.W., Washington, D.C. 20005-4707
RAND URL: http://www.rand.org/
To order RAND documents or to obtain additional information,
contact Distribution Services: Telephone: (310) 451-7002;
Fax: (310) 451-6915; Internet: order@rand.org

The West's growing interest in the Caspian Basin and NATO's increasing concern with challenges on its periphery raise an important question for the Atlantic Alliance as it ponders its future role, commitments, and security responsibilities: Given the nature of the West's security interests in the Caspian and Central Asia regions and the potential threats to those interests, what role should NATO play in a broader Western security strategy for the area?

A great deal of what has been written and said in the West about the Caspian has lacked perspective. Many observers of the contemporary Caspian scene have become intoxicated with the region's potential energy riches and the jockeying for influence among several major powers and international oil companies. The images that have been conjured up of a new "great game" often serve to obscure rather than clarify reality. As a result, many Western views of the Caspian over the past decade have been marked by hype and slogans rather than hard-headed analysis. This report tries to put the south Caucasus and Central Asia into a broader strategic perspective. The authors critically examine NATO's interests, priorities, capabilities and constraints, and the political, economic, cultural, and security forces shaping the regional security environment. After carefully weighing the benefits of deepening the Alliance's involvement in the region against the risks and costs, the authors suggest that NATO should see the region, in general, more as a potential quagmire than as a strategic vacuum waiting to be filled.

This study is part of a larger project on the implications of the changing strategic environment in and around Europe for the United

States and NATO. The project was sponsored by the Commander-in-Chief, U.S. Air Force in Europe, and by the Deputy Chief of Staff for Operations, Headquarters, United States Air Force. It was conducted in the Strategy and Doctrine Program of RAND's Project AIR FORCE. This study should be of particular interest to NATO planners, officials in the U.S. government and Western countries involved in making policy toward Central Asia and the south Caucasus, and, more broadly, anyone interested in the implications of post–Cold War geopolitical dynamics for U.S. military planning and operations.

PROJECT AIR FORCE

Project AIR FORCE (PAF), a division of RAND, is the United States Air Force's federally funded research and development center (FFRDC) for studies and analyses. It provides the Air Force with independent analyses of policy alternatives affecting the development, employment, combat readiness, and support of current and future air and space forces. Research is performed in four programs: Aerospace Force Development; Manpower, Personnel, and Training; Resource Management; and Strategy and Doctrine. Integrative research projects, and work on modeling and simulations, are conducted on a PAF-wide basis.

CONTENTS

FIGURES

During the Cold War, NATO's security concerns focused almost exclusively on the central front of Europe. Other areas were considered of minor importance and Soviet Central Asia and the south Caucasus, in particular, were regarded as a "backwater" of the Soviet Union. Even in the immediate aftermath of the Soviet Union's disintegration in 1991 and the emergence of eight new states in the former Soviet south, Central Asia barely intruded on the geopolitical consciousness of most Western officials. In fact, many in the West were content to give Russia a more or less free hand in dealing with the region and its intractable problems.

Since the mid-1990s, there has been a dramatic change in the Western image of the Caspian Sea Zone and Central Asia. Western interest has grown substantially, spurred largely by the desire to exploit Caspian oil and gas resources, the rapidly expanding presence and financial stake of Western oil companies in the Caspian Basin, and the growing perception that instability and conflict in the south Caucasus and Central Asia could have geopolitical reverberations on a much larger scale. The United States is now a major trade partner of several countries in the region and has played a more active role in trying to mediate ethnic disputes there. NATO has expanded military contacts with several Caspian states through the Partnership for Peace (PfP) program, and is playing a growing role in helping these countries with the reform of their armed forces, including, most recently, in Turkmenistan. The leaders of Caspian states travel regularly to Washington and other Western capitals, where they are given royal treatment, and the leaders of all the countries in the former Soviet south attended NATO's 50th anniversary Washington

Summit in April. Indeed, the pendulum has swung so far in the opposite direction that some observers now describe the Caspian Basin as an area of "vital" American and Western interest and put its energy potential in the same category as the Persian Gulf's.

NATO's shift in emphasis from the Cold War mission of territorial defense to a broader range of threats reflects a growing awareness that conflict and instability on and beyond NATO's borders represent the most serious challenge to Alliance security interests in the post–Cold War security environment. Indeed, this outward-looking orientation may explain NATO Secretary General Javier Solana's February 1997 statement that "Europe will not be completely secure if the countries of the Caucasus remain outside European security." More significantly, the Alliance's interest in projecting stability around NATO's periphery is reflected in the Alliance's new Strategic Concept. This statement of the Alliance's new roles and missions, which was approved at the April 1999 Washington Summit, defines NATO's purpose in the post–Cold War era as extending stability and security throughout the Euro-Atlantic region. The Strategic Concept, moreover, acknowledges that achieving this purpose can be adversely affected by developments on the periphery of this region. In explaining the Alliance's new purpose, NATO officials have stressed that the Euro-Atlantic region encompasses all the members of the Euro-Atlantic Partnership Council (EAPC)—in other words, all the countries in the Caspian region and Central Asia.

The countries of the Caspian region and Central Asia have likewise reached out to NATO to bolster their security and reduce their dependence on Russia. In particular, Azerbaijan and Georgia have launched a major campaign to expand their military and security relationships with the Alliance. Azerbaijan has invited the United States, NATO, or Turkey to establish a military base on Azeri territory and has hinted that Azerbaijan should be considered for NATO membership for its role as a bulwark against Russian expansionism. Baku has also offered to assign a small contingent of forces under Turkish command for NATO peacekeeping forces in Bosnia. Both Azerbaijan and Georgia have expanded military contacts, training, and exercises with Turkey, and have proposed cooperation with NATO in protecting oil pipelines. In fact, Georgia has requested NATO technical assistance in the protection of these pipelines. Finally, the Georgian parliament recently passed two resolutions endorsing Georgian membership in NATO while at the same time requesting Russia to withdraw its forces from Georgian military bases. Together, these developments have stirred fears in Moscow and elsewhere that NATO seeks to extend its military hegemony over the Caspian and that the Alliance will eventually deploy forces there, given the huge energy resources of the Caspian region and its location in the heart of Eurasia.[1]

NATO's strategic transformation, the changing geopolitical environment in the Caspian Basin, and the desire of countries there to rely on NATO to counterbalance Russia raise the issue of whether Western security interests are of sufficient importance to warrant NATO's military engagement and what form, if any, this involvement should take. For both geopolitical reasons and energy security, the West has a tangible and growing stake in promoting the security of the Caspian region as well as the stability, sovereignty, and independence of the new states that emerged from the collapse of the Soviet Union earlier in the decade. Because of its location in the heart of Eurasia, conflict and disorder in the south Caucasus and Central Asia could threaten the security and stability of surrounding areas, including NATO member Turkey, and affect the domestic evolution and external geopolitical alignments of such key countries as Russia, China, Turkey, Iran, Pakistan, India, and Afghanistan.

The Caspian Basin, moreover, has the potential to emerge as an alternative source of energy supplies over the coming decades, reducing pressure on Persian Gulf oil to meet the growing global demand for oil and tempering upward pressure on oil prices. At the same time, however, the competition for influence in the region and control over Caspian oil and gas resources and pipeline routes—which many observers have labeled the new "great game"—has the potential to foment instability and conflict.

More important, developments in the Caspian region could affect Russia's ongoing political and economic transition and its relations with the West. In the past few years, Russian hegemony in the former Soviet south has given way to a more open and fluid multipolar balance of power. How Russia reacts to the continuing erosion of

---

[1] See David Stern, "East-West Fault Lines Deepen in Caucasus as NATO Meets," *Agence France-Presse*, April 23, 1999.

its exclusive sphere of influence could affect its internal evolution. In particular, the emergence of strong, stable, and independent Western-oriented states along Russia's southern borders would discourage a revival of Russian neo-imperialism and a commitment of scarce Russian resources to preserving Russia's position.

Developments in the Caspian Basin are likely to present a severe test for the West's and NATO's ability to promote their larger security agenda. The newly independent republics along Russia's southern border are potentially weak and unstable. Over the next 10–15 years, the Caspian states will face serious internal and intraregional threats to their stability and security. These include regional, tribal, ethnic, and clan disputes; severe poverty and economic hardships; growing disparities in income distribution; immature political institutions, civil societies, and national identities; environmental degradation; political repression; lack of viable succession mechanisms for the orderly transfer of power; rapid population growth; mass urbanization; conflict over land, water, and energy and mineral resources; ethnic separatism; pervasive corruption, crime, and cronyism; and an almost complete breakdown in the delivery of basic social services.

In other words, the Caspian states generally suffer from the usual problems of "weak" or "failed" states. One or more of them could lose the capacity to govern effectively and maintain order. However, while the crises and instabilities resulting from the loss of national authority could threaten Western interests and perhaps engender pressure for NATO involvement in crisis management/peacekeeping, it is far from clear that these interests are "vital" or that the West and NATO would have the will, capabilities, and resources to exert significant influence.

To a degree that is consistent with the modest interests it has in the region, the West can and should increase its engagement there and fashion a comprehensive long-term strategy aimed at promoting democratic and economic development and ameliorating the root causes of conflict and instability. The main elements of such a strategy include

- continued Western political and financial support for construction of multiple pipelines to transport Caspian oil and gas supplies;

- increased assistance to Caspian states to foster democratic and market reforms; respect for minority rights and the rule of law; improved health care, education, and family planning; and enhanced capabilities to combat illicit drug trafficking, control porous borders, manage refugee problems, respond to natural disasters, and repair environmental and ecological damage;

- greater American and European support for Organization for Security and Cooperation in Europe (OSCE) and UN efforts to prevent and resolve ethnic and territorial conflicts in the region; and

- increased emphasis, with respect to both resources and programs, on Uzbekistan, Azerbaijan, and Kazakhstan, the three states with the greatest capability to affect regional dynamics.

Notwithstanding much of the hyperbole that has accompanied the discovery of energy resources and the fascination with the struggle for geopolitical position, the West does not have "vital" interests at stake in the Caspian region. Military instruments are, in general, suited to protecting and advancing only a subset of those interests the Alliance does have.

- First, most of the region's conflicts are likely to remain localized, and those with the potential to spread (e.g., civil war in Tajikistan) have little strategic import for NATO. For the foreseeable future, it is unlikely that a regional conflict in the volatile south Caucasus would lead to attacks on Turkish territory, although the long-term possibility that ethnic irredentism could spark military conflict between Iran and Azerbaijan bears watching because of its potential to precipitate Turkish military assistance to Azerbaijan.

- Second, although Russia will remain the dominant power in the region for some time, neither it nor any other regional or outside power will have the capability to establish regional hegemony, given the multiplicity of actors on the Caspian scene and their inherent limitations. Consequently, while many of the Caspian states will maintain some degree of dependency on Russia, which will at times constrain their freedom of action, Russia will lack the strength to achieve Commonwealth of Independent States (CIS) reintegration, prevent Western inroads in the region, or assert a diktat over the policies of the Caspian states.

- Third, the Caspian is unlikely to become a major source of oil for at least ten years. Even if the region achieves its maximum potential, which remains uncertain, its contribution to global energy supplies will be modest, given the small size of Caspian reserves compared to the global oil reserve base, the high cost of extraction and production, and trends in the global oil market (e.g., low oil prices) that are likely to further reduce the profitability of Caspian oil development. As a result, the West is unlikely to become "dependent" on Caspian oil and thus a threat to Caspian oil supplies probably would not warrant NATO military intervention to restore access.

- Fourth, although there is general Western support for the independence of states in the region, there is little likelihood of an Alliance consensus that preserving the independence and territorial integrity of the Caspian states is critical to Western security. Most NATO countries continue to regard Central Asia and the south Caucasus as tangential to the Alliance's core security interests. In light of the deep divisions within NATO over military operations in the Balkans, it is illusory to believe that the Alliance could reach consensus on similar undertakings in the Caspian. Hence, it is extremely unlikely that NATO will extend security guarantees to any of the Caspian states or offer prospective membership in the Alliance, even to countries that might eventually meet NATO's guidelines for admission.

- Fifth, at least for the next decade, the Caspian states (and substate actors) will generally lack the means and the motivation to acquire weapons of mass destruction (WMD). Moreover, even if states in the region acquired WMD in response to unanticipated security threats, it is unlikely that such weapons would pose a threat to NATO's security. For these reasons, it is unlikely that NATO would extend its counterproliferation mission to the Caspian region, particularly with respect to developing the operational capabilities to deal with specific threats.

- Sixth, although it is likely that parts of the Caspian region will be afflicted with conflict and disorder, the prospect of an independent NATO peacekeeping or crisis management role is remote for the foreseeable future. Russia is virulently opposed to such a role, especially in light of the intense anti-NATO sentiment sparked by the Alliance's bombing of Kosovo, and Moscow is in a position to play the role of spoiler. Indeed, there would be substantial opposition within the Alliance to a NATO peacekeeping operation in the Caspian, even in the unlikely event it enjoyed Russian support, given the limited nature of Western interests in the region, the prospects of disproportionately high costs and casualties in potentially open-ended peacekeeping operations, and the escalatory risks of introducing NATO's forces.

- Finally, while there are plausible circumstances under which a radical, anti-Western brand of Islam could engulf the region, such a prospect remains unlikely. Further, the internal dynamics of Caspian societies, rather than Western actions, will determine the future of militant Islam there. The use of NATO military force would be an inappropriate and ineffective response to combat the spread of radical Islam.

Thus, several key principles emerge as guideposts for developing a road map for NATO in the Caspian region:

- The most serious threats to the security and stability of the Caspian states are internal. Western policy should therefore focus on resolving the political, economic, and social challenges that could breed internal conflict and instability. Western interests in the Caspian region will be best protected by political, economic, and energy security measures to promote democracy and market economies. Success in carrying out this long-term strategy will require patience, resolve, commitment, and resources—there are no quick fixes to the daunting challenges confronting regional governments.

- NATO's most relevant military instruments in the region will be advisory assistance, training, and guidance in helping the military establishments of the Caspian states to restructure along Western lines. The United States and NATO should consider a policy of differentiation in extending such aid: Those countries that demonstrate a real commitment to democratic reform merit greater support. It is difficult to imagine circumstances that would warrant direct military intervention by NATO forces across the full spectrum of potential conflicts.

- U.S., Western, and NATO resources are limited. Western objectives for the region must therefore be fairly modest.

- Although Russia is weak and distrusted throughout most of the region, it nonetheless is likely to remain an influential power and, in some cases, the predominant power in the Caspian for some time. Hence, its legitimate interest in security and stability along its borders should be accommodated. But Russia should recognize that the establishment of stable, prosperous, and independent states along its periphery is in its interests. Consequently, NATO initiatives in the region, if sensitively implemented, need not work at cross-purposes with a strategy of engaging Russia on matters of concern to the West.

- Given higher priorities and U.S. and allied commitments in other regions of the world, the Alliance should avoid creating expectations among the Caspian states that NATO's interests are so important that it will extend security guarantees vis-à-vis Russia. NATO is probably not prepared to deliver on such promises.

If these considerations are taken into account, the emerging security environment in Central Asia and the south Caucasus is likely to have minimal implications for NATO's security commitments or military plans, activities, and force posture. The growing and important Western interests in the region—preventing a single power from gaining regional hegemony, preserving access to energy, preventing the spread of WMD and the spillover of conflict to important countries—are not endangered in the current security environment.

Because there is no direct role for NATO forces to play in responding to the threats and opportunities in the changing Caspian security environment over the next decade, the Alliance does not need to consider major changes in force planning or force structure resulting from regional developments. To be sure, NATO's peacetime engagement (e.g., training exercises, deployments, military-to-military contacts, etc.) has value in demonstrating Western interest, bolstering the independence of the Caspian states, and promoting regional security cooperation. However, resources are limited and many NATO countries harbor serious reservations about raising the Alliance's military and political profile in the region. NATO's peacetime military activities may carry the downside of creating false expectations about the Alliance's security commitment to the region and inciting a Russian backlash. Accordingly, the United States and NATO should proceed cautiously in expanding military relations with the Caspian states and involve Russia as much as feasible in the planning and implementation of these activities.

Nonetheless, the possibility cannot be ruled out that Russia could get peacekeeping "fatigue" in the Caspian and turn to other organizations, including the UN, OSCE, and NATO, to shoulder some of this burden. Should this happen, NATO could face requests to provide units or assets for peacekeeping operations. Such operations could include airlift operations in support of disaster relief or humanitarian intervention, sanctions enforcement, monitoring of demilitarized zones, military activities along borders, cease-fires, and disarmament agreements, and the deployment of a Macedonia-type peacekeeping force. In all these contingencies, the United States Air Force is likely to face demands on combat aircraft and other specialized units such as airlift, early warning, and intelligence assets. However, until Russia softens its attitude toward a NATO role in Central Asian peacekeeping operations, any NATO planning for such contingencies should only be undertaken as part of a broader dialogue with Russia and the OSCE.

In sum, NATO faces serious limitations on its ability to project influence in the region and solve the most difficult challenges facing the Caspian states. The key objectives of Western policy should be to promote democratic reform, market economies, and nation-building to help mitigate the root causes of conflict and instability. Simply put, NATO's interests in the Caspian and the threats to those interests are not commensurate with the Alliance aspiring to play a major security role in the region. Inasmuch as the Alliance lacks the collective interest, will, capabilities, and resources to assume responsibility for Caspian security, a U.S.-led coalition of willing countries rather than NATO should assume primary responsibility for securing Western objectives there.[2]

In light of these considerations, as well as the Alliance's more pressing priorities on its immediate eastern and southern periphery, deepening NATO engagement in the Caspian region should not command a high priority in terms of resources, planning, or forces. In view of the West's limited interests and leverage in the region and

---

[2]See Richard Sokolsky and Tanya Charlick-Paley, "Look Before NATO Leaps into the Caspian," *Orbis*, Spring 1999, pp. 285–297.

the dangers of NATO overextension, the Alliance should focus its military assistance efforts on promoting restructuring and training, while resisting new commitments and security responsibilities in the Caspian region.

ACKNOWLEDGMENTS

Although the authors alone are responsible for this report's content, we are grateful to many of our RAND colleagues for their advice and support. First and foremost, the authors wish to thank David Ochmanek, Ian Lesser, and Zalmay Khalilzad for their guidance on both the direction and substance of the report. Other RAND colleagues who provided helpful comments on previous drafts include David Gompert, C. Richard Neu, F. Stephen Larrabee, Stuart Johnson, Robert Levine, Robert Nurick, Peter Ryan, Michele Zanini, Thomas Szayna, Gregory Treverton, Mark Burles, and Marten van Heuven.

A number of other individuals also contributed their time, talent, and expertise to review our work. Graham Fuller and Rajan Menon provided thorough and thoughtful critiques of the report. The research and preliminary results of this report were presented to an advisory council in May and August 1998, and our work benefited greatly from the advice and suggestions of that council. We are particularly indebted to Ambassador Robert Hunter, Stephen Hadley, Hans Binnendijk, and Major General Donald Peterson.

Finally, Jeanne Heller and Shirley Lithgow provided invaluable assistance in editing, coordinating, and preparing the manuscript for publication.

Chapter One

INTRODUCTION

The dissolution of the Soviet Union in 1991 and the emergence of the independent states of Central Asia (Kazakhstan, Kyrgyzstan, Tajikistan, Turkmenistan, and Uzbekistan) and the south Caucasus (Armenia, Azerbaijan, and Georgia), coupled with vast oil and gas resources around the Caspian Sea Basin, have increased the geostrategic importance of this region. The Caspian Basin has the potential to emerge as an additional source of energy supplies over the coming decades, and could therefore reduce pressure on the Persian Gulf to meet the growing global demand for oil and dampen upward pressure on oil prices. The states of Central Asia and the south Caucasus, moreover, are generally eager to reduce their dependence on Russia and to develop political, economic, and security relations with the outside world. The emergence of strong, stable, and independent Western-oriented countries along Russia's southern borders would discourage a revival of Russian neo-imperialism, and thus advance the West's broader goal of seeing Russia adopt a non-expansionist and responsible foreign policy.

At the same time, however, the states of the former Soviet south are potentially weak and unstable, and the region is vulnerable to centrifugal forces. Over the next 10–15 years, the Caspian states will face serious internal and intraregional threats to their security and stability as they navigate the difficult transition to modern, post-independence nation-states. These challenges (to name but a few) include regional, tribal, ethnic, and clan disputes; severe poverty and economic hardships; growing disparities in income distribution; underdeveloped political institutions, civil societies, and national identities; environmental degradation; political repression; lack of

1

viable succession mechanisms for the peaceful transfer of power; rapid population growth; mass urbanization; conflict over land, water, and energy and mineral resources; ethnic separatism; and pervasive corruption.[1] In short, the Caspian states generally suffer from the usual problems of "weak" or "failed" states that could lose the capacity to govern effectively and maintain order unless their governments are able to meet the basic expectations of their populaces.

Moreover, the Caspian region is the object of an intense competition for influence and access to oil and gas resources among external powers that could threaten the security of states in the region, foment instability, and provoke military intervention. Because of the region's central geographic location and potential energy prospects, large-scale conflict and instability could threaten the stability and security of much of the Eurasian continent. As Graham Fuller has noted, particularly at stake are

- the future domestic evolution of Russia, Turkey, China, Afghanistan, India, and Pakistan,

- the prospects for cooperation or conflict among Turkey, Russia, China, Iran, Afghanistan, India, and Pakistan,

- the formation of new blocs, alliances, and coalitions among the states in and around central Eurasia, and

- Iran's position in the region and its relationships with the West, Russia, and other key neighboring countries.[2]

From NATO's standpoint, therefore, the independence of the Caspian states, as well as their internal evolution and external orientation, presents both opportunities and dangers that could have implications for the Alliance's security interests, tasks, and military requirements. Stability in the south Caucasus, in particular, is critically important because of its common border with Turkey and the

---

[1]For a cogent discussion of the myriad challenges facing the states of the Caspian region, see Shireen T. Hunter, *Central Asia Since Independence*, The Washington Papers, #168, Center for Strategic and International Studies, Washington, DC, Praeger Press, Westport, CT, 1996.

[2]Graham E. Fuller, *Central Asia: The New Geopolitics*, RAND, R-4219-USDP, 1992.

possibility that future rounds of NATO enlargement could include countries (e.g., Romania, Bulgaria, and possibly Ukraine) that would bring the south Caucasus even closer to NATO's borders. If conflict in the region draws Turkey in, the potential exists for wider NATO involvement. Moreover, chronic violence or instability could precipitate Russian, Chinese, or other outside military intervention. Under these circumstances, the West could perceive a growing challenge to important interests and perhaps even pressure for crisis management, peacekeeping, or military intervention.

This study examines the emerging security environment in Central Asia and the south Caucasus and its implications for NATO and the West. Chapter Two discusses Western strategic interests and objectives in the Caspian region. Subsequent chapters examine threats to these interests and opportunities for Caspian energy development and Western energy security. The final chapter discusses the implications of these security trends for NATO's strategy, plans, security functions, and force posture.

WESTERN OBJECTIVES AND INTERESTS IN THE CASPIAN REGION

Primarily because of geopolitical and energy security reasons, the Caspian region is receiving increasing attention from the West. Extensive, but still largely unexplored, energy resources are concentrated in the Caspian Sea area and the countries of Kazakhstan, Azerbaijan, and Turkmenistan. Given the expected increase in world energy demand over the next 15 years, access to these supplies would benefit Western energy security. Moreover, the competition for control over these resources could have a major impact on the geopolitical landscape of Eurasia and the domestic evolution and foreign policies of such key states as Russia, China, Turkey, and Iran.

With an area roughly half the size of the United States and a population of nearly 72 million, the states of the Caspian region border on Russia, Turkey, China, Afghanistan, and Iran (see Figure 1), and their native populations have strong ethnic, cultural, and religious ties that transcend national borders. By 2010–2015, if current demographic trends continue, the population of the Caspian region could exceed 100 million. In light of its location in the heart of the Asian continent, instability, conflict, and crises in the region could have negative repercussions on a larger scale, including conflict between Russia and Caspian states; ethnic separatism in Afghanistan, Pakistan, Iran, and western China; conflict between Russia and China, Turkey, or Iran; and conflict between the Caspian states and Turkey, Iran, or China.

Although there are many possible alternative futures for the countries of Central Asia and the south Caucasus, it is not difficult to

Figure 1—The Caucasus and Central Asia

describe the scenario that best serves Western interests: a stable, secure, and prosperous region of independent, sovereign, democratic,
free-market countries that respect human rights, the rule of law, and
the rights of minorities and are successfully meeting the basic economic and social needs of their populations.[1] Yet, for most Caspian
states, this rosy scenario of the region's future is not realistic in the
face of the myriad threats to stability and peace. Indeed, as one
prominent specialist on Central Asia has observed, the possibility
cannot be ruled out that the area will become a zone of instability
and crisis and perhaps even descend into chaos.[2] Thus, the key

---

[1]Robert Cullen, "Central Asia and the West," in Michael Mandelbaum (ed.), *Central Asia and the World*, Council on Foreign Relations, New York, 1994, pp. 144–145.

[2]Martha Brill Olcott, "The Caspian's False Promise," *Foreign Policy*, Summer 1998, p. 96. A potentially serious time-bomb waiting to explode is the inability of governments to meet the rising expectations for improved living standards generated by promises of future energy profits. For a discussion of this possibility, see Rajan

questions for NATO are whether, given the nature of the Alliance's security interests, these threats and challenges would require any changes in the Alliance's military missions, security responsibilities, plans, and force posture. Put simply, how important are Western security interests in the Caspian Basin, and to what extent might the use of NATO's military assets be required to prevent or respond to threats to these interests?

Against this backdrop, the West has the following strategic objectives and interests in the region:

- First, by supporting the independence and sovereignty of the Caspian states, prevent any single country from establishing hegemony over the region.

- Second, gain and maintain access to the region's energy resources.

- Third, reduce the likelihood of civil war or intrastate conflict in key states of the region.

- Fourth, impede the proliferation of weapons of mass destruction.

- Fifth, discourage the spread of militant, anti-Western Islamic movements.

- Sixth, prevent the spillover of conflict into areas that are of concern, principally Turkey and the Persian Gulf.

It is not enough, however, to simply state NATO's objectives in the region. The Caspian cannot be viewed in isolation; rather, it must be put in the context of present and potential U.S. and Alliance commitments. The United States already has extensive security commitments and military deployments in Europe, the Persian Gulf, and northeast Asia. Our military forces are stretched thin in carrying out their missions and these commitments are unlikely to diminish anytime soon; to the contrary, they are likely to grow (in the Balkans, for example). Moreover, projected increases in defense spending are unlikely to close the gap between our capabilities and commitments.

Menon, "Treacherous Terrain: The Political and Security Dimensions of Energy Development in the Caspian Sea Zone," *National Bureau of Asian Research*, Vol. 9, No. 1, February 1998. For a similar perspective, see Robert Ebel, *Energy Choices in the Near Abroad*, Center for Strategic and International Studies, Washington, DC, 1997.

Our European allies face similar constraints on their willingness and ability to accept new security undertakings. European governments remain preoccupied with threats in Europe and the challenges associated with achieving greater political and economic unity as well as a common foreign and security policy. In short, their finite resources and energies for the foreseeable future will be devoted to deepening and expanding the European enterprise. European governments will therefore have little stomach for undertaking new commitments that do not bear on this objective.

In sum, there is considerable reluctance, even as NATO expands the definition of its role, to undertake security responsibilities beyond Europe's borders. Alliance peacekeeping operations in the Balkans have already strained NATO's political cohesion and military capabilities. Consequently, the policy choices the United States and NATO will confront in the Caspian Basin will be made in the context of other commitments and limited resources. Western governments no doubt understand that the region has the potential to place new and overwhelming military, economic, and political burdens on the West. Before NATO embarks on ambitious new ventures in the region, it will need to carefully consider whether any expanded responsibilities are in line with its interests and capabilities in a vast and remote region that presents multiple sources of conflict and instability.

Chapter Three

INTERNAL AND REGIONAL THREATS TO NATO INTERESTS

The governments of Central Asia and the south Caucasus face a kaleidoscope of challenges as they each navigate the transition to modern, independent, and stable states. Most of these problems emanate from internal dynamics within each state that limit their ability to ensure stable and legitimate governments for the population. These are weak states characterized by repressive personalistic rule with strong ethnic divisions and gross maldistribution of income and resources. These problems are compounded by the weakness of intraregional cooperation on a host of shared economic, security, and social problems. Together, the weakness of these states and the absence of multilateral cooperation threaten Western strategic interests in maintaining regional stability, a favorable balance of power, and access to energy supplies. These trends suggest that the next 10–15 years could witness the emergence of large-scale instability and conflict and the possibility of state collapse.

INTERNAL THREATS TO STABILITY

The emergence of truly independent and stable states in Central Asia and the south Caucasus is impeded by the magnitude of challenges they face. These weak states must resolve conflicts over both the redistribution of political power and the control over economic resources, in an environment where ethnic tensions and other social, cultural, and religious cleavages have been exacerbated by previous colonial (Soviet) policies.[1]   The very weakness of these states increases the role of subnational identities in internal politics. This, in turn, poses further threats to the stability and integrity of states in the region.

Perhaps the most important factor threatening the long-term security and stability of Central Asia and the south Caucasus is the absence of institutionalized mechanisms for the resolution of the inevitable expression of economic, ethnic, or political grievances and ambitions.   None of the countries has come very far in creating coalition or power-sharing arrangements between key groups of elites, much less opposition parties.   Few have acknowledged mechanisms for the transfer of power.   Dissatisfaction with an incompetent or corrupt regime is also likely to foster serious internal political instability as rival alternative groups jockey for power.[2]   This is apt to become a very real issue as the current leaders age and do not cultivate successors.

The Caspian area is characterized by enormous ethnic, linguistic, cultural, tribal, and religious diversity.   Soviet-era borders arbitrarily divided ethnic groups into one or more states and placed dissatisfied minorities within states.   These conditions make separatism and irredentism possible, as witnessed by the struggles in Abkhazia and Karabakh and the low-level conflict in the Fergana Valley between Uzbekistan and Tajikistan.   In addition, within many of these states, the continuation of Soviet ethnic policies of titular and preferred national status, which has led to political stability in the short term, threatens long-term stability by inflaming tribal, political, and eco-

---

[1]These policies include the preferential treatment of settler populations or the designation of often minority titular nationalities as well as the arbitrary delineation of borders.   See David Laitin's work on Central Asia; Graham Fuller, "Central Asia: The Quest for Identity," *Current History*, Vol. 93, No. 582, April 1994, pp. 145–149, for discussion of titular nationalities; and Ashley J. Tellis, Thomas S. Szayna, and James A. Winnefeld, *Anticipating Ethnic Conflict*, RAND, 1997, for discussion on the potential for ethnic strife and catalysts for mobilization.

[2]Enders Wimbush, "Central Asia and the Caucasus: Key Emerging Issues and U.S. Interests," March 14, 1998, unpublished paper prepared for the RAND Conference on Security Dynamics in Central Asia and the Caucasus; Valery Tsepkalo, "The Remaking of Eurasia," *Foreign Affairs*, Vol. 77, No. 2, pp. 107–126; and Zbigniew Brzezinski, "The Eurasian Balkans," *The Grand Chess Board*, Basic Books, NY, 1997, pp. 123–150.

nomic grievances.[3] In Kazakhstan, for example, among those most alienated are the majority of the urban population as well as minority groups in the resource-rich western part of the country. The situation is reminiscent of Nigerian ethnic and economic policies.

ECONOMIC DEPRIVATION AND SOCIAL DISCONTENT

The collapse of the Soviet Union and the transition to independent economies have resulted in an enormous economic disruption for all of the former Soviet republics. The result of the collapse is that the economies and societies of Central Asia and the south Caucasus have experienced rapid declines in their incomes and purchasing power.

Under the Soviet Union, the populations of the Caspian region were the beneficiaries of a comprehensive package of social services. As a consequence, educational, health, and welfare standards were well above those of their non-Soviet neighbors. With the end of Moscow's subsidization of these programs, social services have fallen at the same time as real Gross National Product (GNP) has dropped. Since 1989, GNP for the former Soviet Union (FSU) overall has fallen on average about 33 percent as measured in World Bank Atlas exchange rates or compared with U.S. purchasing power parity. It seems likely that stabilization will be accompanied by stagnation for a few more years before production slowly begins to increase. Furthermore, within this generally depressing picture, there are great regional differences. The worst cases are those states—Georgia, Tajikistan, Azerbaijan, and Armenia[4]—that have had to spend a percentage of their income on the conduct of war.

---

[3]In many of the Central Asian countries, particular clans, often numerically in the minority, were favored by the Communist Party for local leadership positions and continue to have a disproportionate hold on power in the newly independent states. In Kazakhstan, for instance, power has increasingly become concentrated in the hands of President Nazarbayev and his clan. See Nurbulat E. Masanov, "The Clan Factor in Contemporary Political Life in Kazakhstan," translated by Mark Eckert, *Johnson's Russia List*, February 20, 1998.

[4]Geoffrey Jukes, "Central Asia: The Soviet Heritage and Future Relations with Russia," *Russian and Euro-Asian Bulletin*, July 1997. In 1996, Georgia reported a GNP that had fallen to only 20 percent of its 1989 level. Tajikistan's GNP has declined to 28–35 percent of 1989 levels. Azerbaijan is reporting GNP at 27–36 percent of 1989 levels. Nonwarring states such as the Kyrgyz Republic and Uzbekistan reported only 20–50 percentage reductions in GNP. Reliable data are not available for either Turkmenistan

These declines are not unexpected, given the enormous challenges that each state has had to face. They are, however, significant. A period of prolonged impoverishment is likely to have an unfavorable effect on interethnic and interclan relations in these societies because the economic burden is not evenly spread across ethnic groups. The future failure of governments to radically change these economic and social conditions will make a mockery of the (perhaps unrealistic) promises that these governments have made to their citizens based upon the expectation of enormous oil wealth. Oil revenues may placate popular grievances, but are more likely to increase the gap between rich and poor and fuel anger over this relative deprivation.

DISTRIBUTION OF WEALTH: REALITIES AND EXPECTATIONS

In the Caspian states, the redistribution of economic wealth and power across ethnic and social groups has been complicated by the promise of oil and gas revenues. If low prices or difficulties with extraction or delivery significantly decrease regional oil revenues, social tension and even revolt against the government is likely to result from unmet and postponed societal expectations. This will be especially true in states, such as Turkmenistan, that have postponed reforms in the expectation of vast energy revenues.

However, dangers exist even if the most optimistic projections for oil revenues are fulfilled. In other developing countries, oil revenues have increased the gap between rich and poor, between the cities and the countryside, and between modernists and traditionalists. This is troublesome since the oil-rich Caspian states have used the promise of future oil revenues to placate their populations and legitimatize the political status quo. Azerbaijan represents the most extreme version of this pattern.[5]

---

or Kazakhstan. It is highly likely that the scale of underreporting in all of these statistics is large and that there has been a distinct shift to unregistered household economic activities. For statistics on GNP in the region, see Stephen Wheatcroft, "Revisiting the Crisis Zones of Euro-Asia, Part Two: The Crisis Zones in 1997," *Russian and Euro-Asian Bulletin*, April 1997, pp. 1–4.

[5]John Thornhill and Carlotta Gall, "Stability Rooted in Presidential Hands," *Financial Times*, March 3, 1998, pp. 11–12.

Thus, a key question for the future of the energy-rich Caspian states is how long the population will continue to be mollified by promises of future economic prosperity. Conflict may occur if oil revenues are either as high as projected but not distributed to the population in tangible ways, or if they are significantly lower, prompting popular frustration and rage. The potential for conflict will be exacerbated if the population continues to perceive that their government is corrupt or incompetent in the administration of the revenues.[6]

The states of the south Caucasus face a related internal economic and political challenge. Because of their location on existing or planned oil pipelines (see Figure 2), ethnic groups in these states have been emboldened in their demands for political and economic autonomy. For example, the strategic location of Abkhazia· and Karabakh has attracted outside sponsors and increased the states' military capabilities, giving their separatist struggle more credibility.

REGIONAL SOURCES OF CONFLICT AND INSTABILITY

Weak states, combined with internal threats, could spawn regional conflict and instability as their weaknesses spill over into neighboring states. Porous borders allow the spread of conflict, terrorism, and illicit commerce in drugs. State weakness and emerging power imbalances raise the capacity for large-scale bloodshed, the direct involvement of Russia as a combatant, and the redrawing of territorial boundaries in a way that destabilizes the regional balance of power. The most dramatic potential boundary revisions include a carving up of Tajikistan with northern Tajikistan joining Uzbekistan and southern Tajikistan joining with northern Afghanistan to form a new state; integration of northern Kazakhstan with the Russian Federation; and territorial shifts between Armenia and Azerbaijan if they renew their conflict over Nagorno-Karabakh. There are several potential regional conflicts that would be particularly serious challenges to the balance of power, regional stability, and Western access to regional resources.

---

[6]For a discussion of this danger, see Laurent Ruseckas, "Energy and Politics in Central Asia and the Caucasus," *National Bureau of Asian Research Analysis*, Vol. 1, No. 2, July 1998, pp. 16–17.

SOURCE: Rajan Menon, "Treacherous Terrain: The Political and Security Dimensions of Energy Development in the Caspian Sea Zone," *National Bureau of Asian Research Analysis*, Vol. 9, No. 1, February 1998, p. 5.

Figure 2—Existing and Potential Oil and Gas Routes from the Caspian Basin

The biggest wild card in the region is Uzbekistan, a country that has alternated between a conflictual and cooperative approach in its relationships with its neighbors. Uzbekistan benefits from its geographic position in its quest to be the dominant regional power. It is the only Central Asian state that shares a border with all of the others. It is also the most populous state in the region. Finally, there are significant Uzbek populations in other Central Asian states. The Uzbek government has declared that it has the duty to protect the rights and safety of these populations. It has further angered and scared its neighbors by making historical claims to parts of Kazakhstan, Kyrgyzstan, Turkmenistan, and Tajikistan, including the fertile Osh region and Fergana Valley.

The Fergana Valley spreads over southern Kyrgyzstan, eastern Uzbekistan, and northern Tajikistan. The valley is one of the most densely populated and agriculturally rich regions in Central Asia. It has been a source of bitter contention among all three states. The borders of the three countries zigzag through this area with no regard for tribal/ethnic borders, leading to strong irredentist feelings. Almost the entire Uzbek population in Kyrgyzstan lives in this valley (552,000 Uzbeks live with 1.2 million Kyrgyz). In addition, the war in Tajikistan has driven refugees and freedom fighters into this area of Kyrgyzstan. With a collapsing economy, frustrations have mounted and resentment between ethnic groups is high.[7]

Depending upon the fate of the peace accords in Tajikistan, the Uzbek-dominated portion of Tajikistan situated in this valley may seek to secede. Antagonism between Uzbeks and Tajiks was inflamed at the beginning of the civil war in 1992 when Uzbeks living in Tajikistan joined a faction attempting to reinstitute a neo-Soviet regime. Since the conclusion of a cease-fire and coalition agreement, this tension has abated somewhat. However, instability continues to threaten the agreement Russia is active in brokering. Uzbek secession in Tajikistan would increase the pressure on Kyrgyzstan, a country extremely weak in military power and dependent upon the Russians for territorial security. It would also have the effect of reorienting Tajikistan. A truncated Tajik state would be likely to look to Afghanistan to strengthen its weight against Uzbekistan. Finally, the future relationship between Uzbeks and Tajiks is uncertain. Uzbekistan contains within its territory two of the most important Tajik

---

[7]Valery Tsepkalo, "The Remaking of Eurasia," *Foreign Affairs*, Vol. 77, No. 2, March/ April 1998, pp. 107–126. See especially the section on Central Asian flashpoints.

cultural centers, Bukara and Samarkand. If Tajikistan becomes a more attractive place to live, Tajiks residing in Uzbekistan may seek the return of these lands to Tajikistan.[8]

Uzbekistan's major rival for regional economic and political power is Kazakhstan. Both countries have openly espoused their goal to create a new common Central Asian home. Both countries have also aggressively competed for economic leadership.[9] The only real possibility of a large-scale military clash in the region is between these two pivotal states. However, the military capabilities and assets of these two countries are currently mismatched.[10] On its own, Kazakhstan is not likely to be able to ensure its security against a much stronger Uzbek military. Kazakhstan's military capabilities have suffered from a lack of government funds and commitment. By contrast, the strength of the Uzbek military may be attributed to the large stock of both ground and air force equipment, much of it newer-generation systems, that it inherited with the breakup of the Soviet Union. Defense spending has been kept at a reasonably high level and the Ministry of Defense has been energetically engaging in military reform over the last four or five years, which has increased both military morale and performance. However, the military equation is not simply bilateral, since Russia acts as a brake against military confrontation by ensuring Kazakh national security. Kazakhstan, like all of the countries in the region except Uzbekistan and Azerbaijan, relies on Russia to help patrol its borders. Thus, Russia plays an important role in Central Asia as a buffer and source of stability. However, the Russian-Kazakh relationship is also uncertain.

A potent lingering identity conflict in the region is between the two major ethnic groups in Kazakhstan: the ethnic Kazakhs and the Rus-

---

[8]Martha Brill Olcott, *Central Asia's New States: Independence, Foreign Policy, and Regional Security*, United States Institute of Peace, Washington, DC, 1996.

[9]On the historical roots and current manifestations of this conflict, see Martha Brill Olcott, "Ceremony and Substance: The Illusion of Unity in Central Asia," in Michael Mandelbaum (ed.), *Central Asia and the World*, Council on Foreign Relations Press, New York, 1994, pp. 17–46.

[10]Unless otherwise noted, data on military capabilities are drawn from *Kazakhstan, Kyrgyzstan, Tajikistan, Turkmenistan, and Uzbekistan: Country Studies*, Glenn Curtis (ed.), Federal Research Division of the Library of Congress, March 1996; and O'Malley and Solchanyk (1997).

sians. In Kazakhstan, only the three southernmost provinces are populated principally by Kazakhs and other Turkic groups. The ethnic balance in the north is rapidly changing, however, both through conscious government policy and differential population growth rates. Although the numerical impact of these policies has been gradual, their psychological effect has been strong.[11] These changes make the ethnic Russians feel increasingly threatened economically and politically, causing them to call for Russian diplomatic and possibly military intervention on their behalf.

The tension between Russians and Kazakhs within the republic has not yet reached a boiling point. The current Russian government is committed to the rights of Russians in the near abroad but is also sensitive to the need for close commercial and security cooperation with Kazakhstan. Many Russians have simply chosen to emigrate to Russia rather than struggle in Kazakhstan. However, the potential for secession of the north remains. Much depends on the nature of future Russian regimes.

The fragmentation of Kazakhstan, should it occur, would have geopolitical significance. If a Russian-dominated northern Kazakhstan should break away from the rest of the republic, the balance of power in the region would certainly shift dramatically. A rump Kazakh state might invite Uzbek intervention if, freed of the need to balance Russian interests against its desire for relationships with its southern neighbors, it began to play a more radicalized role.[12] Kazakhstan also might become so weak as to become irrelevant, leaving Uzbekistan as the sole regional Central Asian power.

The promise of oil revenues has regional as well as domestic implications. Significant revenues have the potential to change the strategic calculations among adversaries, such as Azerbaijan and Armenia, tempting Azerbaijan to launch a military challenge to the fragile status quo. The dispute over Nagorno-Karabakh, the Armenian enclave in Azerbaijan, while now dormant, has the potential to destabilize the south Caucasus. Owing to their decisive military vic-

---

[11]See Curtis (1996); Martha Brill Olcott, "Central Asia's Post-Empire Politics," *Orbis*, Spring 1992, pp. 253–268.

[12]Olcott (Spring 1992).

tory over Azerbaijan in 1993–1994, the Armenians have been largely successful at achieving their goals. The Republic of Nagorno-Karabakh is de facto independent, although that independence has not formally been recognized by any other country. However, President Aliyev of Azerbaijan is calculating that Armenia will compromise and return the area to Azerbaijani control with the highest level of autonomy to prevent the complete isolation of the country from planned oil pipeline routes and thus economic revenues.[13]

In the event that no compromise is reached, the conflict has the potential to escalate. The current military in Armenia has benefited from military transfers from Russia (and possibly China) to further its fight for the independence of Nagorno-Karabakh.[14] Azerbaijan, by contrast, has a weak military but is not dependent upon the presence of Russian troops for its security. However, as oil revenues in Azerbaijan increase, the military may remedy this imbalance by importing weaponry from allies in the Middle East. In anticipation of this possibility, some high-ranking Armenian officials have hinted at the possibility that Armenia might launch a preemptive strike before its military advantage is lost to the Azeris.

The combination of ethnic, economic, security, and leadership challenges outlined above confronts each state in the region with significant threats to its stability and prosperity. Securing the cooperation of other states would lessen the difficulties of coping with these problems, many of which, such as illicit drug trafficking and environmental pollution, are transnational in character. That said, developing habits of multilateral cooperation and institutionalizing mechanisms for such cooperation present a formidable challenge. This is an inherently difficult task, but is especially challenging for

---

[13]Thornhill and Gall (1998), pp. 11–12.

[14]On July 16, 1998, Russian Defense Minister Igor Sergeev announced the intention to add modern weaponry to the Russian arsenal deployed in Armenia. Russian military hardware based in Armenia is used by both Russian and Armenian troops. Any new deliveries would add to the estimated U.S. $1 billion worth of weapons transferred by Moscow to Armenia—presumably for dual use—in 1994–1996. Those transfers are of concern also to the United States and NATO in the context of the Conventional Forces of Europe (CFE) treaty. See "Plan to Station More Russian Arms in Armenia Alarms Azerbaijan," *Jamestown Monitor* (electronic version), July 20, 1998; "Azerbaijan Accuses China of Selling Rockets to Armenia," *Radio Free Europe/Radio Liberty Newsline*, Vol. 3, No. 97, Part I, May 19, 1999.

weak states. The experience of the Caspian states to date in forging such cooperation is not encouraging, but some modest progress is likely, even in the security field.

As the Commonwealth of Independent States (CIS) has slowly unraveled as an effective vehicle for economic or military-political cooperation in the region, a number of regional associations in Central Asia and the south Caucasus have emerged as alternatives to CIS integration. However, real progress in this direction has been limited by institutional weaknesses in these nascent organizations, rivalries between states and their leaders, the lack of experience in true consultation and coordination, and the proliferation of organizations. As a result, no single forum has yet to emerge to coordinate and cooperate on practical steps to address the spectrum of common challenges.

The proliferation of organizations has contributed to their ineffectiveness. Membership across the organizations is overlapping, making coordination extremely difficult. Lacking experience in compromise and consultation, states in the region have done little to develop formal structures for implementing multilateral initiatives. Furthermore, efforts to foster effective regional cooperation have been hampered by Russian obstructionism. Russia has been particularly adept at exploiting and intensifying existing rivalries between Uzbekistan and Kazakhstan, the two major sources of leadership in Central Asia.[15]

Regional security cooperation has also been impeded by the ambivalence these states feel toward each other and toward Russia. Although Azerbaijan, Uzbekistan, and Georgia have pulled their militaries out of the CIS, Russia has continued to dominate security arrangements through bilateral treaties with individual states. At the same time, many of the states have concerns that an exclusive reliance on Russia might jeopardize their emerging sovereignty and independence. The most promising, albeit fledgling, alternative security arrangements are the association of Georgia, Ukraine, Uzbekistan, Azerbaijan, and Moldava, known as GUUAM, and the Central Asian Peacekeeping Battalion (CENTRASBAT). Both of these

---

[15]Olcott (1996), p. 145.

organizations, however, rely on outside forces to guarantee security. In Central Asia, no state is willing to rely on the security guarantees that the Central Asian states could offer one another. There may even be a lack of will to cooperate. One expert on the region argues that Central Asians remain convinced that their regional security interests would be best protected if Moscow or, even better, a group of disinterested states were to participate in the process of resolving their problems.[16]

Not surprisingly, the fear of a Taliban victory in Afghanistan and the spread of Islamic extremism beyond the Afghan border has galvanized the Central Asian states, except Turkmenistan, into intensified consultations on regional security cooperation. It remains to be seen, however, whether such concerns will lead to concrete forms of cooperation. Moreover, the warnings issued by Central Asian leaders to the Taliban have explicitly stressed the inviolability of CIS borders, a not-so-veiled threat that Taliban efforts to spread its brand of Islamic extremism to Central Asia would be met by a firm CIS (read Russian) response.

Indeed, the Central Asian states seem unlikely in the near future to be able to handle serious threats to their stability on their own. Institutions are still tenuous and largely ad hoc. No organization has emerged that could provide an effective substitute for the Russian-dominated CIS. Although the region is likely to rely on Russia as its primary security guarantor, organizations dominated by Russia are not likely to teach these countries how to compromise and consult as equals. There is a role for the West to foster these habits and skills. To the extent that these nascent regional organizations increase multilateral cooperation and security, they reduce the likelihood of either regional hegemony or widespread instability.

THE REGION'S FUTURE AND CHALLENGES FOR THE WEST

The multiple sources of conflict and instability in the Caspian region portend a quagmire if the West assumes responsibilities out of kilter with its strategic interests. Unfortunately, at both the state and re-

---

[16]Olcott (1996), p. 43.

gional level, institutional weakness and ineffectual leadership are the norm. The weakness, or even failure, of local states is likely to lead to internal and cross-border conflict. Existing regional security institutions will not be equipped to respond to these challenges and are likely to call for outside assistance.

However, as will be discussed later, these small-scale conflicts are not likely to be resolved effectively by the application of force by either Western powers or nearby regional actors. NATO and the West should do what they can, within the constraints they face, to shape an environment hospitable to Western interests in the stability, security, and independence of these states. However, given limited Western resources to meet likely challenges to these interests, NATO members will need to prioritize their military, political, and economic assistance to the areas of greatest strategic importance. The preceding analysis suggests that NATO will have the greatest strategic interest in the stability and security of Azerbaijan, Uzbekistan, and Kazakhstan. The second tier of countries would include Georgia and Turkmenistan, although, as discussed later, Georgia may merit greater attention because of the commitment it has shown to true democratic reform.

Chapter Four

THE THREAT OF REGIONAL HEGEMONY

The geopolitical importance of the Caspian region does not stem solely from its energy potential. Whether or not the area emerges as a major energy producer, its central geographical location, the considerable potential for regional instability and internal and interstate conflict, and the competition among external powers for influence all suggest that events in the region will shape the balance of power in Eurasia and the geopolitical order that will supplant Russian hegemony. The West, therefore, will have an interest in preserving peace, order, and stability in the south Caucasus and Central Asia.

Over the next decade, Caspian states will make fundamental choices about their national identity, interests, external relationships, and place in the world.[1] Further, these choices will be made within an extremely fluid environment characterized by an active and increasing competition for influence among several outside powers, including Russia, Iran, Turkey, China, and the United States and its European allies. Each of these countries will be pursuing its own agenda and this dynamic will present the states of Central Asia and the south Caucasus with opportunities and challenges in charting their future.

The dissolution of the Soviet Union aroused widespread apprehension that the existence of fragile and unstable states in Central Asia and the south Caucasus would create a "strategic vacuum" and ignite an intense and destabilizing competition among outside powers to fill it. However, predictions that the region would fall prey to the

---

[1]Graham E. Fuller elucidates these choices well in *Central Asia: The New Geopolitics* (1992).

domination of an outside power have thus far proved to be unduly alarmist. To be sure, the presence and influence of outside powers will continue to grow. That said, most of the states in the Caspian and Central Asia have proven adept at increasing their independence and maneuvering room by playing off outside powers against each other. Indeed, there is no "power vacuum" for outside powers to fill and a multipolar regional balance of power is evolving, which will make it extremely difficult for any single country to establish regional hegemony.[2]

The discussion below focuses on the main external actors—Russia, China, Turkey, and Iran. However, other regional actors also hope to cultivate close ties with the Central Asian and Caucasus states. Of these, perhaps the most interesting are Pakistan and India. For both of these countries, strong relations with Central Asian states represent important political opportunities and regional leverage. However, these countries lack the capability to exert major influence over regional events and are therefore touched on only lightly.

RUSSIA: THE ONCE BUT NOT FUTURE HEGEMON

Russia continues to see Central Asia and the south Caucasus as vital to its security interests. Since the mid-1990s, these interests, which are enshrined in a September 1995 presidential edict on Russian policy toward the CIS, have been defined as establishing an exclusive Russian sphere of influence, minimizing the expansion of foreign presence and influence on CIS territory, preventing or containing local wars, and protecting ethnic Russians.[3] Russia has relied on three main tools to advance these interests: (1) integration of the CIS under Russian domination; (2) the use of military, economic, and political leverage to subordinate the independence of the Caspian states to Russia's interests; and (3) international recognition of an exclusive Russian-led CIS peacekeeping role and Russia's "special powers" as

---

[2]This is the conclusion reached, among others, by the International Institute for Strategic Studies. See "Caspian Oil: Not the Great Game Revisited," in *Strategic Survey 1997/98*, International Institute for Strategic Studies, London, 1998, pp. 22–29.

[3]"Strategic Policy Toward CIS Published," *Foreign Broadcast Information Service Daily Report: Central Asia SOV-95*, September 28, 1995, pp. 19–20.

guarantor of peace and stability in the space occupied by the former Soviet Union.

From the vantage point of Western policy and interests, the key questions are: (1) whether Russia will continue to pursue these ambitions and, if so, whether Moscow will be successful in preserving Russian supremacy, and (2) what measures are available to NATO and the West to counter Russian actions that threaten the independence of the Caspian states and access to the region's energy resources.

Russia's expansive conception of its security interests in the Caspian region, which many observers have labeled "neo-imperialist," is reflected in several different ways:[4]

- Russian military doctrine stresses regional threats and local conflicts, the need to improve the mobility and deployability of Russia's conventional forces to deal with conflicts on Russia's periphery, the imperative of protecting Russians in the "near abroad," and the importance of preventing other countries from gaining a foothold in the region. Further, senior Russian military officials have expressed the view that Central Asia's borders are Russia's as well, and that because of the vulnerability of the area to Islamic fundamentalism Russia needs to maintain a strong military presence to prevent the Caspian states from falling victim to Islamic extremism. As one expert on Russian military policy has observed, the Russian military thinks of Central Asia as a buffer zone along its southern border and has adopted a forward defense strategy predicated on the belief that the defense of Russia's borders starts at the CIS border in Central Asia.[5]

- High-ranking Russian civilian and military officials have repeatedly emphasized that Russia's security can best be protected by establishing a sphere of influence in the former Soviet south and by defending Russia's special rights, interests, obligations, and

---

[4]For an excellent discussion of Russian military attitudes toward Central Asia and the South Caucasus, see Rajan Menon, "In the Shadow of the Bear: Security in Post-Soviet Central Asia," *International Security*, Vol. 20, No. 1, Summer 1995, pp. 149–181.

[5]See John W.R. Leppingwell, "The Russian Military and Security Policy in the Near Abroad," *Survival*, Vol. 36, No. 3, Autumn 1994, p. 77.

responsibilities in the region. Russian officials have repeatedly proposed that the United Nations grant the CIS the status of an international organization and confer on the CIS an exclusive monopoly over peacekeeping responsibilities on Russia's southern periphery.

- Russians across the political spectrum defend Russia's right to use force to protect the rights of the Russian diaspora, an attitude reflected in the Russian government's long-standing proposal that Russians living in Central Asia should be granted dual citizenship.

- The Russian government mounted an intense and ultimately successful effort to revise the Conventional Forces in Europe (CFE) flank agreement to allow Russian forces to exceed regional subceilings, thereby increasing the forces Russia could bring to bear on its southern periphery. The Russians have also successfully pressured some countries to reallocate their shares of CFE equipment entitlements to Russia.

- The Russians have frequently exploited local conflicts to deploy peacekeeping forces and to use the presence of these units to extract agreements from local states permitting Russia to maintain bases, border guards, and forward-deployed forces.

- Russia has played hardball to maintain its preeminent position in the region, prevent the spread of foreign influence, muscle its way into energy development consortia, and retain exclusive control over energy pipeline routes. Heavy-handed attempts at blackmail, coercion, subversion, and violence include interventions on behalf of Abkhazian separatists in Georgia (which the Russians exploited to extract basing agreements from Tbilsi), military support of Armenia in its conflict with Azerbaijan (which the Russians used to leverage Baku into joining the CIS), attempts to install more pliant regimes in Azerbaijan and Georgia when these governments resisted Russian pressures for tighter CIS integration, and numerous cutoffs of oil and gas exports from Azerbaijan, Turkmenistan, and Kazakhstan.[6]

---

[6]Russia's "neo-imperialist" activities in the former Soviet south have been richly described by several authors. See, in particular, the following articles: Stephen J. Blank, *Energy, Economics, and Security in Central Asia: Russia and Its Rivals*, U.S.

Russia's policies in Central Asia and the south Caucasus have had mixed results. Russia remains the predominant external power and has had limited success in establishing a partial sphere of influence throughout the former Soviet Union. Many post-Soviet Caspian states remain dependent on Russia for trade, energy supplies, military equipment and training, and internal stability and external security, and Moscow maintains strong political, economic, and military ties to several states.[7] Further, the Russians have exploited their leverage and the weakness of Caspian states to extract military and economic concessions, including basing rights, participation in energy projects, and favorable decisions on pipeline routes. Russia maintains a basing structure and military presence in the region and continues to lead regional peacekeeping operations and international efforts to mediate regional conflicts. In the south Caucasus, the area of greatest concern to Moscow, the Russians have established important footholds in Armenia and Georgia: bases, installations, and security treaties. Russia's arrangements with Armenia, in particular, are especially far-reaching and Moscow has recently transferred more advanced conventional weapons to Armenia.[8] Finally, the Russians have achieved a partial degree of CIS integration, most notably the creation of a customs union with Belarus, Kazakhstan, and Kyrgyzstan.

At the same time, there are numerous signs of Russia's shrinking influence and the erosion of its once hegemonic position.[9]

- **CIS integration.** As previously noted, the development of CIS political, economic, and military integration is a central goal of

---

Army War College, Carlisle Barracks, PA, 1995; Ariel Cohen, "The New 'Great Game': Pipeline Politics in Eurasia," *Eurasian Studies*, Vol. 3, No. 1, Spring 1996, pp. 2–15; Michael P. Croissant, "Oil and Russian Imperialism in the Transcaucasus," *Eurasian Studies*, Vol. 3, No. 1, Spring 1996, pp. 16–26; and S. Frederick Starr, "Power Failure: American Policy in the Caspian," *The National Interest*, No. 47, Spring 1997, pp. 20–31.

[7]Rajan Menon (February 1998), p. 10.

[8]See Tomas Valasek, "Arms Buildup or Arms Race?" *Weekly Defense Monitor*, Center for Defense Information, January 28, 1999.

[9]The authors would like to acknowledge the contribution of RAND colleague Abraham S. Becker to the discussion of CIS failings. These are described further in "Russia and the Caucasus-Central Asia States: Why Is Moscow Floundering?" paper prepared for the RAND Conference on Security Dynamics in Central Asia and the Caucasus, March 1998.

Russian foreign policy. Nonetheless, CIS cooperation has been plagued from the outset by intramural disputes, conflicting agendas, lingering rivalries and mistrust, and, most important, Russia's lack of resources. As a result of these centrifugal forces, the CIS has not evolved into a coherent and effective regional organization—a major setback for Russia in light of Moscow's goal of using a rejuvenated CIS under Russian leadership to restore Russia's great power status. The most dramatic example of the decrepit state of the CIS is the inability or unwillingness of CIS members to implement more than a handful of the roughly 1300 CIS integration agreements.

Russia's hopes for CIS integration have also been dashed by the refusal thus far of Azerbaijan, Uzbekistan, and Turkmenistan to join CIS political and economic structures. These ambitions were dealt a further blow by the recent decisions of Azerbaijan, Georgia, and Uzbekistan to withdraw from the CIS Collective Security Treaty. Consequently, the limited integration that has been achieved to date is largely informal and tenuous; although some CIS states remain dependent on Russia militarily and economically, most of this cooperation has been achieved within a bilateral rather than multilateral framework. In short, the CIS resembles a "Potemkin" organization and the prospects are dim that Russia will be able to rescue it from near-certain oblivion.

- **Energy development and transport.** Russia's ability to control energy production and export is declining in several areas. After years of heavy-handed Russian pressure, Moscow has recently moved closer toward accepting the position of Azerbaijan and Kazakhstan (and occasionally Turkmenistan) that Caspian Sea resources should be divided into national sectors. Russia has also lost its exclusive monopoly over pipeline routes with the recent completion of an oil pipeline and the opening of a new rail route that will allow Azeri oil exports to bypass Russia. Kazakhstan and China have concluded an agreement on the construction of a major pipeline across Chinese territory which, if implemented, would further erode Russian control over the flow of Caspian oil. Finally, some of the more extreme Russian demands for equity shares in oil development consortia have been rebuffed and Lukoil, the giant Russian oil company, has lost bids entirely on some other projects.

- **Search for alternative powers.** In varying degrees, the Caspian Basin states have enjoyed success in reducing their dependence on Moscow and diversifying their economic, political, and military relationships. Trade with Russia is declining as the Caspian states develop commercial ties with non-CIS countries, including Turkey, Iran, Pakistan, China, Korea, Japan, Israel, Germany, France, Italy, and the United States. Scores of multinational companies, led by the oil and gas industry, have poured huge investments into the region, and the rapidly expanding regional transportation network, spearheaded by the European Union (EU) effort to create an east-west transportation corridor, promises to increase links between the Caspian states and the outside world. High-level diplomatic contacts between Caspian states and Western countries have increased dramatically. All the states of Central Asia and the south Caucasus have joined NATO's Partnership for Peace (PfP) program and some have sought the assistance of outside countries in restructuring and professionalizing their armed forces.[10]

More recently, Azerbaijan has shown interest in a proposal for the so-called GUUAM countries to form a joint battalion to protect planned oil pipelines that would operate independently of the UN or the CIS.[11] In March, Azerbaijan, Georgia, and Ukraine signed a defense protocol and the following month they conducted a joint military exercise to protect oil pipelines—developments that further underscore the decline of both Russian power and the Russian-backed CIS as the major security organization in the FSU.[12]

The future of Russia's policy toward the Caspian region remains uncertain, but the possibility cannot be ruled out that Moscow may shift to a more cooperative and less confrontational policy, given Russia's deep economic and financial woes and the political and

---

[10]Roger Kangas, "With an Eye on Russia, Central Asian Militaries Practice Cooperation," *Transition*, Vol. 2, No. 16, August 9, 1996.

[11]Valasek (1999).

[12]Paul Goble, "New Moves on the Caucasus Chessboard," *Radio Free Europe/Radio Liberty Daily Report,* April 16, 1999.

economic currents sweeping the region. At least in the short run, Russia's traditional military, security, and intelligence elites will likely cling to the view that conflict and instability along its southern border, coupled with the expansion of Western influence, especially in the south Caucasus, pose a threat to Russian security interests. These nationalist and conservative elements within Russia's foreign policy establishment are likely, therefore, to continue advocating an assertive policy of defending Russia's interests in maintaining primacy in the region and thwarting inroads by outside powers.

Nonetheless, given Russia's resource constraints and internal problems, as well as the growing assertiveness of the Caspian states, Moscow faces a huge and perhaps irreversible gap between its ambitious objectives and the means available to achieve them. Simply put, as many commentators have noted, Russia lacks the military and economic wherewithal, as well as the political competence and ideological legitimacy, to maintain its supremacy in the region and to prevent other states and international organizations from gaining increased influence and access.[13]

Moreover, it is by no means certain that Moscow will continue to pursue a hard-line "neo-imperialist" policy in the Caspian region. Despite the consensus that developments in the southern CIS states are important to Russian security and that Russia should remain engaged in the region, differences have emerged within Russian decisionmaking circles over how Russia should define and pursue its interests there. As one leading Central Asian analyst has put it, Russia has been confused over what constitutes Russian interests in Central Asia and how to pursue them.[14] Indeed, these divisions within Russia's foreign policymaking process have complicated Russia's ability to formulate and implement a coherent strategy toward the Caspian region.[15]

---

[13]See, for example, Stephen J. Blank, "Russia's Real Drive to the South," *Orbis*, Summer 1995, p. 324.

[14]This is the view of Lena Jonson of Britain's Royal Institute of International Affairs, as cited in Stuart Parrott, "Central Asia: Russia Reduces Its Role," *Radio Free Liberty/Radio Liberty Daily Report*, January 26, 1998.

[15]See Sherman Garnett, "Russia and the Former Soviet South," *Central Asia Monitor*, No. 6, 1998.

Russia's traditional foreign policy and security establishment continues to espouse a muscular policy toward the region that relies largely on old-fashioned Soviet-style tactics of confrontation, intimidation, and coercion to protect Russian equities. At the same time, some of its new "capitalist" class and increasingly powerful oil, gas, and financial interests support a more conciliatory policy based on cooperation with the West and accommodation with Caspian states. These interest groups are dependent on access to Western markets, investments, and technology and are primarily interested in integration with the West and market reform. Accordingly, they are motivated primarily by a desire to earn profits from participation in oil and gas development rather than geopolitical considerations, and have little taste for flouting international norms and the West to maintain exclusive control over pipeline routes.[16] Moreover, these elites harbor serious reservations about CIS reintegration because of the additional resource burdens it would place on Russia as well as the risks reintegration would pose to expanding Russia's economic relations with the West.

Russia's ability to realize any "neo-imperial" designs it may have on the region will be handicapped by these discordant voices and the fragmented nature of Russian foreign policymaking.[17] A fundamental problem is the lack of any clear consensus on Russian strategy, objectives, and priorities in the "near abroad." Hence, while many Russian officials share a general interest in preserving Russian preeminence in the Caspian region, they disagree over the form this preeminence should take and how to achieve it, especially what price Russia should be willing to pay in support of an assertive policy. In addition, as many observers have noted, the Russian decisionmaking

---

[16]On how Russia's oil and gas interests influence Russian policy in the Caspian region, see Igor Khripunov and Mary Matthews, "Russia's Oil and Gas Interest Group and Its Foreign Policy Agenda," *Problems of Post-Communism*, Vol. 43, No. 3, May–June 1996, pp. 32–49. It is important to note, however, that given their inability to compete with Western oil companies, these interests are forced to rely on the Russian state to leverage them into deals.

[17]Robert Freedman, "Russia and Iran: A Tactical Alliance," *SAIS Review*, Vol. 17, No. 2, Summer-Fall 1997, pp. 97–99. For a more general discussion of the competition among various political and economic factions in the making of Russian foreign policy, see Michael McFaul, "A Precarious Peace: Domestic Politics in the Making of Russian Foreign Policy," *International Security*, Vol. 22, No. 3, Winter 1998/1999, pp. 5–35.

process is characterized by disorganization, severe factionalism among the ruling elites, fragmented and confused lines of authority, a plethora of semi-autonomous bureaucratic fiefdoms, and a lack of centralized planning, coordination, and political control.[18] For these reasons, many Russian actions toward the Caspian region since 1992—for example, independent Russian military activities in Georgia's separatist conflicts and the open dispute between the Russian Foreign Ministry and Lukoil over development of Caspian Sea oil— are best explained by lack of foreign policy coordination, rather than the result of an organized and centrally directed effort to establish a Russian sphere of influence.

The eventual outcome of this schism remains uncertain. Events in the region, of course, will have a major influence on Russian behavior, as will the nature of Russia's regime and the extent of its economic power in the years ahead. That said, recent Russian actions suggest that the center of gravity within Russia's decisionmaking structure may be shifting, albeit slowly and fitfully, toward the advocates of a softer policy toward the region. A growing number of Russian officials, for example, admit that Russian assertiveness has been counterproductive and express frustration over Russia's inability to achieve its economic and geopolitical objectives in the Caspian. A recent series of Russian moves to mediate a resolution of ethnic conflicts in the south Caucasus and the change in Russia's position on the legal status of the Caspian Sea are other indications of a moderation of Russian policy.[19]

---

[18]For an in-depth look at the disorganization and incoherence in Russian foreign policy, see Scott Parrish, "Chaos in Foreign Policy Decision-Making," *Transition*, May 17, 1996, pp. 30–31.

[19]A full treatment of the complicated legal issues related to the status of the Caspian Sea is beyond the scope of this report. Although the delimitation of the sea's boundaries and resources has not been fully resolved, and the situation remains highly fluid, Moscow has moved closer to accepting the position that the Caspian Sea should be divided into national sectors and that each littoral state would have unilateral control over the disposition of resources within its sector. There have been a spate of articles detailing the ongoing negotiations over Caspian Sea delimitation. See, for example, Michael Lelyveld, "Russia: Moscow's New Caspian Policy," *Radio Free Europe/Radio Liberty Report*, April 7, 1998; Merhat Sharipzhan, "Central Asia: New Developments in Russian Caspian Policy," *Radio Free Europe/Radio Liberty Report*, April 17, 1998; John Helmer, "Kazakhstan/Russia: Caspian Oil Disputes Linger," *Radio Free Europe/Radio Liberty Report*, May 13, 1998; and Paul Goble, "Caspian: Analysis from Washington—Pipelines Under Troubled Waters," *Radio Free*

From the standpoint of Western security interests, one long-term trend appears clear: Russia has lost its hegemony over the region and has little hope of restoring its control or an exclusive sphere of influence, because of Moscow's preoccupation with economic problems and other domestic challenges, the costs of an imperial policy and Russia's resource constraints, the lack of domestic support for military adventures in the region, shifting demographic and trade patterns, and firm Western support for the independence of the Caspian states. Thus, occasional Russian demonstrations of muscle flexing on its southern border belie the underlying trend of a steady reduction in Russia's role and influence in the region. At least for the next five to ten years, Russian leverage over most of the Caspian states will decline further, as will Russian influence relative to that of other external powers with regional interests.

Nonetheless, it would be a mistake to write Russia off because of its declining influence. Despite the difficulties Russia has encountered in pursuing an effective and coherent policy toward the Caspian, most Russian elites continue to view an extension of Western influence in the region as a threat to Russian national interests and harbor anxieties about Moscow's declining control there. In addition, many Russian civilian and military officials firmly believe that Russia has a legitimate role to play there as the chief guarantor of stability and security. Despite the occasional rhetoric, a number of CIS states, including Kazakhstan, Tajikistan, and, to a lesser degree, Turkmenistan and Uzbekistan, see Russia as a stabilizing force and fear that Russian disengagement would exacerbate the internal and external challenges they face. Indeed, chaos in the region may draw Russia in, and few states are poised to replace Russia as "peacekeeper."[20]

Europe/Radio Liberty Report, July 10, 1998. For a more extensive discussion of the legal dimensions of the Caspian Sea dispute, see Cynthia M. Croissant and Michael P. Croissant," The Caspian Sea Status Dispute: Content and Implications, *Eurasian Studies*, Vol. 3, No. 4, Winter 1996/97, pp. 23–40. These articles paint a rapidly shifting and, at times, confusing picture of intense maneuvering for position among the parties to the dispute. In the final analysis, however, it is hard to disagree with Paul Goble's view that a formal and definitive resolution of this dispute will prove elusive, setting the stage for endless conflict among the countries and companies involved.

[20]A number of observers of Russian policy toward the Caspian region have a tendency to assume that Russia has achieved its dominant position through raw coercion and intimidation. These analysts appear oblivious to—or are unwilling to admit—the

Equally important, Russia's decline in the Caspian region must be viewed in relative terms. Russia, as Rajan Menon has argued, is neither an omnipotent predator nor a paper tiger.[21] In fact, notwithstanding the contraction of Russian power, Russia remains the dominant power because of the weaknesses of the Caspian states and the constraints on the ability of other outside powers to project influence into the region and to commit resources on a scale sufficient to supplant Russia's predominant role.[22] For better or worse, many states in the region will remain dependent for some time on Russian security guarantees and military assistance and Russia will continue to play a substantial role in shaping political, economic, and security developments.[23]

Thus, while Russia may be irreversibly locked into a long-term process of "involuntary" disengagement from the region, Russian weakness will not necessarily mean Russian passivity.[24] As Zbigniew Brzezinski has observed, Russia will be too weak to reimpose its imperial domination but too powerful to be excluded.[25] For historical, geographic, cultural, ethnic, and strategic reasons, Moscow will try to

---

tangible benefits many of these states accrue through their close association with Moscow. Clearly, Moscow has resorted to unseemly behavior to extend its presence and influence throughout the region, particularly in the south Caucasus. Nonetheless, Russia's relations with the Central Asian states are more complex than popular perception suggests. For a more nuanced and balanced view of the attitudes and policies of these states toward Russia, see Bess A. Brown, "Security Concerns of the Central Asian States," in Jed C. Snyder (ed.), *After Empire: The Emerging Geopolitics of Central Asia*, NDU Press, Washington, DC, 1995; Susan Clark, "The Central Asian States: Defining Security Priorities and Developing Military Forces," in Michael Mandelbaum (ed.) (1994); Roland Dannreuther, "Russia, Central Asia, and the Persian Gulf," *Survival*, Vol. 35, No. 4, Winter 1993, pp. 92–112; and Maxim Shashenkov, "Central Asia: Emerging Military-Strategic Issues," in Jed C. Snyder (ed.) (1995).

[21]Menon (February 1998), p. 10.

[22]Several other analysts share Menon's view of continued Russian primacy in the Caspian region. See, for example, Robert Ebel, *Energy Choices in the Near Abroad: The Haves and Have-Nots Face the Future*, Center for Strategic and International Studies, Washington, DC, 1997; Paul Goble, "Pipeline and Pipedreams: The Geopolitics of the Transcaucasus," *Caspian Crossroads*, Vols. 1–2, Winter 1995–Spring 1997, pp. 3–6; and David E. Mark, "Eurasia Letter: Russia and the New Transcaucasus," *Foreign Policy*, No. 105, Winter 1996–1997, pp. 141–159.

[23]Menon (February 1998), p. 10, pp. 35–36.

[24]Dannreuther (1993), p. 94. Also, Lena Jonson, as cited in *Radio Free Europe/Radio Liberty Daily Report*, January 26, 1998.

[25]Zbigniew Brzezinski, *The Grand Chessboard*, Basic Books, New York, 1997, p. 148.

use Russia's remaining leverage to protect Russian interests in a weak, fragmented, and unstable region.[26] The perception that Russia retains considerable leverage to influence developments in the region is reflected in the growing tendency of Caspian states to try to co-opt rather than exclude Russia from participation in key energy development projects.

CHINA'S LIMITED INFLUENCE

In 1997, China successfully entered the Central Asian oil sweepstakes by securing the rights to develop and transport oil from one of Kazakhstan's major fields. China's success raised alarm in some quarters that the Chinese were bent on establishing hegemony in Central Asia and supplanting American and Western multinational oil corporations.

Such concerns are not without merit. China sees the Caspian region as a major source of much-needed energy resources. Chinese calculations about Central Asian oil supplies are not based on market considerations of cost effectiveness, but on the goal of securing energy resources at any cost; hence, China's plans to construct a pipeline from Kazakhstan to eastern China are political/security rather than economic in character. China may thus contend vigorously in Central Asia to secure energy supplies, including supplying arms for oil. Moreover, China views the United States as a key geopolitical rival in the region, and its policy toward Central Asia is one element of a broader strategy to reduce Chinese vulnerability to U.S. power and to create a multipolar world.[27] Beijing is unlikely, therefore, to embrace the liberal Western agenda of democratization and "globalization" for Central Asia. Similarly, China does not share the commitment to opening the region to liberal global markets or to removing the region's neo-communist regimes from power. Rather, China would prefer to dominate the region to keep a lid on nationalism and the West at bay. In particular, China has no interest in see-

---

[26]See S. Enders Wimbush, "Central Asia and the Caucasus: Key Emerging Issues and U.S. Interests," unpublished paper prepared for the RAND Conference on Security Dynamics in Central Asia and the Caucasus, March 1998, p. 5.

[27]On this point, see Mark Burles, *Chinese Policy Toward Russia and the Central Asian Republics*, RAND, MR-1045-AF, 1999.

ing nationalist governments come to power in Central Asia that might embolden or support the Uighur separatist movement in China.

Nonetheless, it is important to bear in mind that Chinese policy toward Central Asia and the Caspian Basin reflects a complex and subtle set of political and strategic motivations. China's primary objective is to maintain the country's territorial integrity by ensuring that the Xinjiang-Uighur Autonomous Region (XUAR), historically the scene of Turkic and Muslim separatist agitation, remains firmly under Beijing's control. To further this objective, Chinese policy is designed to maintain stability and contain ethnic, religious, and nationalist separatism through economic development.[28] Key to success of this policy is China's ability to forge trade and commercial relationships with the Central Asian countries bordering China, including the development of rail and transportation links and pipeline construction, and to maintain tranquility along the borders between the XUAR and Central Asian republics.

The Chinese, moreover, want to prevent trouble in Central Asia from interfering with Beijing's access to the region's energy resources, including China's potentially vast oil reserves in the Tarim Basin, or from hindering efforts to integrate neighboring Central Asian countries into the Chinese market. As one prominent expert on Chinese energy policy has observed, Beijing's concerns about energy security are a driving factor behind China's forays into the Central Asian oil market. The key to the success of China's strategy for energy security is the cooperation of Russia and Kazakhstan in linking the energy resources and markets of Central Asia to northwest China.[29]

Put slightly differently, Chinese interests, at least in the short term, are primarily negative in character—Beijing is more interested in preventing unwanted developments than in pursuing a grand vision or "master plan" for carving out an exclusive Chinese sphere of influence in Central Asia. China will seek to expand its political and economic influence in those areas adjacent to its borders. Furthermore,

---

[28]See Dianne L. Smith, "Central Asia, A New Great Game?" *Asian Affairs*, Vol. 23, Fall 1996, p. 161.

[29]Gaye Christoffersen, "China's Intentions for Russian and Central Asian Oil and Gas," *The National Bureau of Asian Research*, Vol. 9, No. 2, March 1998, p. 5.

given China's geographic proximity, size, and economic dynamism; cross-border ethnic ties; and the interest of Kyrgyzstan, Tajikistan, and Kazakhstan in reducing their dependence on Russia and developing markets for their own products, Chinese influence and presence in these areas are bound to grow and could eventually result in a dominant Chinese role. That said, the easternmost regions of Central Asia are of significantly less strategic concern to the West. More important, a host of factors limit China's ability, as well as opportunities, to project its influence in the western portions of Central Asia and the south Caucasus. These include:

- China's lack of foreign capital for investment: Tajikistan and Kyrgyzstan lack oil and gas resources and therefore must rely on foreign capital for economic development, particularly in exploiting the region's hydroelectric sources of energy. As a developing country with its own enormous need for capital investment, it is unlikely that China will be able to make vast sums of capital available to these countries—or even to Kazakhstan, where the stakes are higher.

- Kazakhstan's ethnic, economic, and geopolitical orientation: Much of Kazakhstan's oil reserves, manufacturing sector, and mineral deposits are in areas that are close to Russia and contain large Russian populations; moreover, Kazakhstan's economy is still closely integrated with Russia's. In addition, the Kazakhs are cultivating strong energy and economic relationships with a number of countries and multinational corporations whose influence and resources dwarf China's. Consequently, most of the strategically and economically important areas of Kazakhstan will be less susceptible to Chinese economic influence.

- China's remoteness from the heart of Central Asia: Both Uzbekistan and Turkmenistan are physically separated from China. The Uzbeks have their own aspirations to regional domination and thus are unlikely to welcome a significant expansion of Chinese influence. Because of its location and natural gas resources, Turkmenistan is oriented toward developing improved ties with Iran, Turkey, and Azerbaijan. It is hard to visualize an ascendant China in Central Asia if these two countries prove resistant to Chinese political and economic penetration.

- Central Asian threat perceptions: As Roland Dannreuther has observed,[30] the three countries bordering China feel threatened by China and harbor suspicions of long-term Chinese intentions. Moreover, China's penetration of local economies has engendered resentment and hostility. Although recent Chinese actions—especially the settlement of outstanding border disputes—have allayed these fears, an abiding distrust of China will complicate Beijing's quest to expand its influence.

For at least the next five years, Chinese objectives in Central Asia are likely to remain limited and defensive in nature. The focus of China's security policy will be Northeast and Southeast Asia, and Central Asia will be a region of secondary importance, unless there is a major outburst of ethnic separatism and disintegration of public order. Furthermore, China's relationship with Russia and Russia's role in the region will loom large in Beijing's calculations of benefits, risks, and costs as it considers its moves on the Central Asian chessboard. Beijing will almost certainly take Russian sensitivities into account, given the growing importance of their bilateral relationship. Moreover, in many areas, such as maintaining stability and preventing the growth of both radical Islamic fundamentalism and pan-Turkic nationalism, China and Russia share common interests. China would appear to have little incentive, therefore, to risk a rupture in its relations with Russia by pursuing an overly aggressive policy that challenges Russian predominance in the region and is out of proportion to Beijing's limited ends and means. Indeed, China appears content to let Russia take the lead in stabilizing the region, and would move more aggressively only if Russia, because of its weakness, could not play this role.[31] Even under these circumstances, however, Beijing lacks the military, political, and economic capabilities to project influence much beyond its border areas with Central Asia.

That said, over the longer term Chinese success in dominating the region economically would have major political repercussions, and

---

[30]Roland Dannreuther, *Creating New States in Central Asia*, Adelphi Paper 288, Oxford University Press for the IISS, London, 1994, pp. 63–64.

[31]Rajan Menon argues convincingly that China has conceded Russia's preeminent role in Central Asia. See his chapter, "After Empire: Russia and the Southern Near Abroad," in Michael Mandelbaum (ed.) (1998).

would certainly arouse Russian resentment and hostility, if not conflict. Indeed, Russian-Chinese tension in Central Asia is likely to grow in the next decade and could become a flashpoint for confrontation. Even if China is not successful in establishing its domination over the region or making major inroads, there are two other sources of potential Russian-Chinese conflict. First, notwithstanding Chinese calculations, economic development may not solve the Uighur separatist problem; to the contrary, economic advancement might stir up Uighur aspirations as Uighurs develop stronger ties to the countries of Central Asia. Under these circumstances, and depending on the overall state of Russian-Chinese relations, Russia might succumb to the temptation to support the Uighurs to weaken China. Second, within the next decade it is likely that one or more Central Asian states will seek alignment with outside countries (e.g., China, Russia, Iran, Turkey, or India), which will precipitate the formation of hostile blocs within Central Asia. This process of alliance-building, which could pit Uzbekistan and China against Kazakhstan and Russia or China and a "rump" Kazakhstan against Russia (after it has annexed northern Kazakhstan), could increase the risk of war in Central Asia and a Russian-Chinese military conflict, especially if the current neo-communist regimes are replaced by nationalist leaders. Although these problems will be far removed from NATO and the Alliance will wish to keep them at arms length, they will be cause for concern.

Finally, the growth of Chinese influence in the region is not totally detrimental to Western interests and may indeed be of some benefit. Like the United States and its Western allies, China has an interest in containing the spread of radical Islam; reducing the dependence of Central Asian states on Russia; promoting the independence, stability, and economic development of the Muslim republics; transporting the region's oil to international markets; and opening up the economies of the Central Asian states to the outside world. It would be shortsighted and perhaps counterproductive to allow an unreasonable fear of Chinese expansionism in Central Asia to obscure these common interests, which provide a basis for mutual cooperation rather than conflict.

TURKEY'S ELUSIVE QUEST FOR A LARGER ROLE

The end of the Cold War and the demise of the Soviet Union have had a profound impact on Turkey's security environment and national security policy.[32] The disappearance of the Soviet military threat, which Turkey played a central role in containing, elevated the importance of several divisive issues that had been muted by Cold War imperatives. The human rights situation in Turkey and the Turkish military campaign against Kurdish insurgents have been particularly thorny issues that have complicated Turkey's relations with Europe and the United States. Turkish disaffection with Europe has reached new heights, largely because of the EU's continuing rejection of Turkish membership and Turkish perceptions that Europe is indifferent or even hostile to Turkish concerns, especially regarding the Greek-Turkish dispute over Cyprus. Further, a common vision of shared purposes has yet to emerge that might cement a new U.S.-Turkish relationship for the post–Cold war era.[33] Consequently, over the past few years Turkey's ties with the United States and especially Europe have weakened.

Against this backdrop of Turkey's growing disillusionment with its Western connection, the emergence of independent states in the Caspian region presented Ankara with new opportunities and options in an area of growing geopolitical importance, where Turkey felt strong ethnic, cultural, historical, and linguistic bonds. By offering itself as a bulwark against the spread of radical Islam, Turkey hoped to demonstrate its value to both the United States and Europe, and thus reap additional political and economic benefits. Ankara sought to profit economically from the independence of the Caspian states by capturing markets for exports and tapping into the region's oil and gas reserves to meet its own growing energy needs. The independence of the Caspian states offered Turkey an opportunity to renew its sense of national identity and purpose by asserting its leadership within a broader pan-Turkic community.

---

[32]See F. Stephen Larrabee, "U.S. and European Policy Toward Turkey and the Caspian Basin," in Robert D. Blackwill and Michael Stürmer (eds.), *Allies Divided: Transatlantic Policies for the Greater Middle East*, The MIT Press, Cambridge, MA, 1997, pp. 145–146.

[33]For a perceptive exposition of this view, see Zalmay Khalilzad, "Why the West Needs Turkey," *The Wall Street Journal*, December 22, 1997.

The United States urged Turkey to fill the vacuum left by the crumbling of the Soviet empire, in part to serve as a counterweight to Russian and Iranian influence. Many of the Caspian states (and even Russia) saw an expansion of Turkish influence as insurance against the growth of Iranian-led Islamic fundamentalism, and welcomed Turkey as a source of economic and technical assistance, a potential bridge to the West, an outlet for the region's oil and gas, and a counterweight to Russian pressure. Azerbaijan, in particular, was eager to strengthen its ties to Turkey and Ankara was eager to reciprocate.[34]

The widespread support for an enlarged Turkish role in the Caspian region sparked euphoric expectations that Turkey would emerge as the major regional power and the unofficial leader of a broader pan-Turkic community.[35] From 1992 to 1996, Ankara sought to expand trade and investment and Turkey's political, economic, and cultural influence:

- Ankara sought to use its cultural and ethnic ties to the region to promote its secular, democratic, pro-Western, free-market state as an alternative model to Iranian fundamentalism. For example, Turkey actively supported Islam in Central Asia, opened cultural centers and Turkic schools in almost all of the Central Asian states, and agreed to provide training and technical assistance in Turkey to thousands of Central Asian students. Turkish television broadcasts in Azerbaijan continue to provide a means of expanding Turkish cultural influence.

- Turkey has provided $80 million in humanitarian assistance and extended over $1 billion in credits to various countries, including a recent $300 million line of credit to Kazakhstan. In addition, Ankara has invested over $1 billion in Kazakhstan and is participating in 100 joint ventures in Kazakhstan and 22 in Kyrgyzstan in energy, mining, and construction.

Despite Turkey's natural advantages over many of its regional rivals, Ankara's ambitions to rally the states of the south Caucasus and

---

[34]Larrabee (1997).

[35]See Philip Robins, "Between Sentiment and Self-Interest: Turkey's Policy Toward Azerbaijan and the Central Asian States," *Middle East Journal*, Vol. 47, No. 4, Autumn 1993, p. 593.

Central Asia around the cause of pan-Turkic solidarity have gone largely unfulfilled. Following a burst of Turkish activism in the immediate wake of the Soviet Union's collapse, which was followed by a period of declining interest during the rule of the pro-Islamic Welfare Party, Ankara has cautiously pursued its regional agenda and lowered its profile.[36]   Turkey's tempered expectations are attributable to several factors that will continue to hinder Turkish efforts to increase its role and influence in the region:

- First, Turkey's own domestic problems, in particular Kurdish separatism, the growth of Islamic influence, and economic weaknesses, diverted attention away from the region.

- Second, Turkish diplomatic energy in the Caspian region was drained by other more pressing security challenges, including threats to the south from Syria, Iraq, and Iran, instability to the north in the Balkans, and ongoing disputes to the west with Greece over Cyprus and the Aegean.

- Third, Turkey's lack of geographic proximity to Central Asian countries limited Ankara's ability to project influence there.

- Fourth, as it became abundantly clear that cash-strapped Turkey lacked capital for large-scale economic aid and investments, Central Asian countries lost much of their interest in Turkish proposals for regional economic integration.

- Fifth, Turkey's chauvinism and cultural arrogance and its pretensions to leadership of the pan-Turkic cause offended the sensibilities of many Central Asian leaders, especially in the face of fewer common cultural, social, or even linguistic links than many of the parties expected.[37] As one expert on the region has noted, the peoples of the south Caucasus and Central Asia have a strong sense of national pride, and—having suffered for years under the

---

[36]Gareth Winrow is one of many specialists who has commented on Turkish disappointment over its failure to make greater inroads in the south Caucasus and Central Asia. See Gareth Winrow, *Turkey in Post-Soviet Central Asia,* Royal Institute of International Affairs, London, 1995.

[37]Dannreuther (1994), p. 59.

yoke of Soviet colonialism—were not about to become the "little brothers" of Turkey or any other outside power.[38]

- Sixth, as many of the Central Asian countries developed their own relations with Western countries, they felt less need to rely on Turkey as an intermediary with the West.

- Seventh, Turkey's capabilities to project military power are limited, especially beyond the south Caucasus.

- Finally, Ankara remains wary of taking actions, especially in Georgia and Azerbaijan, that might antagonize Russia, a major trading partner and significant source of energy and the only country still capable of bringing heavy military pressure to bear on Turkey.

In retrospect, Turkey's short-term goals and expectations were unrealistic. Although Turkey has raised its profile in Azerbaijan, it has nonetheless been frustrated in its desire to improve relations with Armenia. Moreover, Ankara's ties with Georgia, while growing, are constrained by Georgia's continued military and economic dependence on Russia. Indeed, Russia has enjoyed some success in thwarting a significant expansion of Turkish influence in the region,[39] especially Kazakhstan, and Turkey has been careful to avoid challenging important Russian interests.

That said, Turkish engagement in the Caspian remains substantial, and the long-term prospects are promising for increased bilateral cooperation and a steady, if unspectacular, expansion of Turkish influence, given the ethnic and cultural bonds that exist and the number of young Central Asians who are being trained in Turkey. Turkey is operating on a crowded playing field, however, and it is unlikely that Ankara will emerge as a dominant player, much less attain regional hegemony. For now, accordingly, Ankara has a more realistic appreciation of the difficulties it faces and has trimmed its policies and expectations to fit these realities.

---

[38]See Patrick Clawson, "The Former Soviet South and the Muslim World," in Jed C. Snyder (ed.) (1995), p. 141.

[39]See Suha Bolukbasi, "Ankara's Baku-Centered Transcaucasian Policy: Has It Failed?" *Middle East Journal*, Vol. 51, No. 1, Winter 1997, pp. 80–94.

Nonetheless, Turkey's desire to be a major actor could create problems for the United States and the West, and it would be a mistake to see Turkey as representing United States interests over the longer term. Ankara, for example, may pursue increasingly independent policies that the United States and other Western countries may find difficult to control, depending on the degree of Turkey's disenchantment with the West and whether ideological considerations (e.g., promotion of the Islamic cause) assume a more prominent role in Turkish foreign policy. Moreover, there is a long-term potential for a serious Turkish-Russian clash in the south Caucasus, particularly if Ankara is unable to resist the rising tide of Turkish nationalism and pressure from public opinion and ethnic groups for a more assertive Turkish posture in the region. Still more seriously, there is a longer-term risk that the competition for influence between Turkey and Iran (fueled by the dangers of Azeri separatism), the conflict between Azerbaijan and Armenia, and the clash of rival Islamic and Turkish secularist ideologies could lead to Turkish-Iranian armed conflict in the south Caucasus. A Russian-Armenian-Iranian war against Azerbaijan and Turkey is another plausible scenario.

IRAN: CHIPPING AWAY AT THE MARGINS

In stark contrast to the warm reception given to the Turkish engagement in Central Asia and the south Caucasus, Iran's forays into the region after the collapse of the Soviet empire were met with deep fear and mistrust among the ex-Communist rulers of the Muslim Republics—a hostility reinforced by the widespread perception that Tehran was providing material and financial assistance to the Islamist opposition forces in Tajikistan. In the early 1990s, Iranian-sponsored Islamic fundamentalism was perceived throughout the region as the most serious threat to regional peace and stability.

Since the middle of the decade, however, Iran has had some success in projecting a more positive image, in part because of the realization that Tehran did not have a major hand in supporting the Islamic groups in Tajikistan, and in part because Iran played a responsible role in helping Russia broker a diplomatic settlement of the Tajik civil war and in trying to mediate the Armenian-Azeri dispute over

Nagorno-Karabakh.[40] More important, however, Iran has kept a low profile in the region and Tehran's policies have been pragmatic, cautious, and moderate. Tehran, for example, has not attempted to export the Iranian revolution through propaganda, subversion, terrorism, or inflammatory religious and cultural activities. Instead, Iran has attempted to expand its influence by providing technical and financial assistance, supporting regional economic integration, expanding cultural links, and facilitating the efforts of Kazakhstan and Turkmenistan to develop alternative transit routes for oil and gas.[41]

Although Iran has made limited inroads, several factors will circumscribe Tehran's opportunities for achieving substantial influence and presence in the near term:

- Iran's revolutionary vision, especially its anti-imperialist and anti-hegemony overtones, has broad appeal among all Muslims, including Sunni movements. Nonetheless, many Muslims in Central Asia have little sympathy for Iran's brand of radical Islam.

- Notwithstanding Iran's heightened interest in Central Asia and the south Caucasus and pipeline routes, Tehran's domestic and foreign policy priorities are currently focused primarily on economic reconstruction at home, safeguarding the Iranian revolution against perceived external threats, and asserting Iran's historical claims to regional domination in the Persian Gulf. These preoccupations will consume much of Tehran's energies for the foreseeable future.

- Because of Iran's own ethnic problems, especially unrest among its large ethnic Azeri minority, Iran's stability and territorial integrity could be undermined by the Azeri separatist movement.[42]

---

[40]Dannreuther (1994), p. 61.

[41]This is the conclusion reached by Edmund Herzig in his careful and incisive appraisal of Iranian policy toward Central Asia and the south Caucasus. See Edmund Herzig, *Iran and the Former Soviet South*, Royal Institute of International Affairs, London, 1995.

[42]On Iran's perceptions of threats to Iranian national security emanating from the former Soviet south, see S. K. Sajjadpour, "Iran, the Caucasus and Central Asia," in Ali Banuazizi and Myron Weiner (eds.) (1994), p. 198.

Because Iran lacks the leverage to influence those developments, Tehran relies on Russia for this task.[43]   This dependence, combined with Iran's growing reliance on Moscow for conventional arms and nuclear technology, gives Iran a strong stake in maintaining close relations with Russia, and this co-operation has hindered the expansion of Iranian influence in the region. It is unlikely, therefore, that Iran would take any actions in Central Asia that might cause serious harm to its relations with Russia. That said, Iran's close ties with Russia today are to a major extent a function of U.S. policy to isolate Iran. Once this policy changes (as it may well be starting to do), the Iran-Russia relationship will in all likelihood weaken.

- With the exception of Turkmenistan, Iran does not border any of the Central Asian states, and this lack of proximity makes it more difficult for Iran to project its influence.

- Iran currently lacks the resources to become a major economic actor. As in the case of Turkey, Iran is not in the position to make major investments, and the abysmal performance of the Iranian economy over the past two decades is hardly a model that the Caspian states would wish to emulate. Furthermore, though Iranian technical expertise could aid in the development of Caspian energy, there is little "complementarity" between the economies of Iran and the Caspian states. Iran sees the Caspian as a market for Iranian goods, especially processed agricultural products, wood products, and light industry. Nonetheless, as Patrick Clawson and others have noted, Iran is unlikely to emerge as a major market for Caspian products, and there is a far greater possibility that Iran and the states of the region will become trade competitors rather than partners.[44]

- As long as Iran remains a pariah state and politically isolated, it will be extremely difficult to carve out a major niche for itself as a significant pipeline route.

----

[43]Dianne Smith (1996), pp. 152–153. Her view is representative of the consensus among regional scholars and analysts that Iranian sensitivity to Russian interests in the Caspian exerts a restraining effect on Iranian behavior. For example, see Herzig (1995), pp. 8–10.

[44]Clawson (1995), p. 153.

• As long as the fundamental character of the Iranian government remains unchanged, the leaders and populations of the Central Asian states will remain highly suspicious of Iranian intentions.

Despite these obstacles to Iranian encroachment, the Caspian region enjoys a higher profile in Iranian foreign policy thinking today. Over the long run, Iran will likely play a growing role, especially in Turkmenistan and Tajikistan, for both geographic and cultural reasons. More fundamentally, important mutual interests bind Central Asia and Iran. From the vantage point of the Caspian states, access to Iran's oil pipelines and transportation networks offers an opportunity to break free of Russia's grip and to reap enormous profits from oil and gas exports. From Iran's perspective, close relations with the Central Asian states offer several benefits—breaking out of its international diplomatic and economic isolation, expanding its influence and leadership position within the Islamic world and the Persian Gulf, earning profits from oil and gas transit fees and participation in Central Asian energy projects, containing ethnic and regional conflicts that could threaten Iran's internal stability, and enhancing its international political status.

In sum, for at least the next decade, Iran's strategy toward Central Asia will probably be defensive and cooperative rather than threatening and confrontational.[45] Because Iran has a strong stake in preserving regional stability to minimize the risk of ethnic separatism at home, Tehran will likely behave as a status quo rather than a revolutionary power. The ruling elites in Tehran almost certainly understand that any overt, aggressive Iranian attempt to foment an Islamic uprising—or throw Iran's geopolitical weight around—would be met by strong opposition from Russia, the United States, China, and Turkey. Iran does not currently possess and, for at least the next decade, is unlikely to acquire the military, economic, and political strength to overcome this opposition. Simply put, if Iran could not establish its hegemony over the Gulf Arab states, where Tehran enjoyed many natural advantages, it seems hardly likely that the Caspian zone will fall under Iran's domination. Nevertheless, as long as Iran is excluded from the development and transport of the re-

---

[45]Dannreuther (1994), pp. 61–63.

gion's energy resources, Tehran will try to play the role of spoiler wherever possible.

INDIA AND PAKISTAN

India has ambitions to play a larger role in Central Asia, but it lacks the capabilities to expand Indian influence in any significant way. A key priority for India in Central Asia is to preserve peace and security, reflecting Delhi's fears of the potentially destabilizing consequences of conflict in Afghanistan and civil strife in Central Asia. As a result, India will support the region's secular regimes to contain the spread of Islamic fundamentalism. However, India does not have the military or financial wherewithal to assume major security responsibilities, and must therefore rely on other external powers—Russia or China—to maintain order and security.

India also sees Central Asia as an important arena for trade and investment. However, the Indians, who inherited a lively trade with the Central Asian republics from Soviet times, have encountered obstacles to increasing economic cooperation and have been hampered by lack of funds for investment. Direct access poses another formidable obstacle to India's economic ambitions. Air routes between Afghanistan and Central Asia are insufficient for any major transfer of goods and services and political disintegration and civil war in Afghanistan make overland transit prohibitive.[46]

India views the evolving Caspian security environment through the prism of its rivalry with China and Pakistan. For instance, India is deeply disturbed at greater Chinese inroads in Central Asia and could be tempted to play the Chinese separatism card in Tibet or the Xinjiang/Uighur region to keep China off balance. Moreover, although India has maintained a low profile in Central Asia over the past few years, a more nationalist government could become assertive. Tensions between India and China are also likely to arise over Caspian energy development, since both countries are competing for access to oil and a share in the region's pipeline sweepstakes. In short, India and China are likely to be rivals for influence in Central Asia. This competition will add a new geopolitical dimension to

---

[46]Dianne Smith (1996), p. 156.

their rivalry and, in particular, will only strengthen existing Indian-Russian strategic cooperation.

Pakistan sees economic, political, and strategic opportunities in Central Asia, but confronts many of the same obstacles to expanding its role as India does, particularly lack of direct access and resources for investment. Pakistan has expanded trade with several Central Asian countries and actively promoted Islamic education as well as social, cultural, and religious activities. Pakistan's common ethnic and historical roots with Central Asians notwithstanding, Pakistan has made only limited economic inroads in the region.

In sum, while Pakistan and India are important actors in the shifting regional economic and security arrangements, both countries lack the capabilities to exert major influence over developments in the region. Both countries, however, see Central Asian states as potential allies in their conflict with each other. Thus, an increasing rivalry between Pakistan and India is likely to be played out in their regional policies.

*   *   *   *   *   *   *   *   *   *

Several key trends and implications emerge from this examination of the policies of the major external powers in the Caspian region: First, there will be increasing competition for influence, most notably growing Russian opposition to U.S./Western inroads, heightened Russian fears of Chinese economic penetration, and the tendency of states to support their oil companies as they maneuver for position. Second, a multipolar balance of power is taking shape that helps preclude any single country from attaining regional hegemony. The major external actors are too weak to impose their hegemony yet strong enough to successfully oppose the hegemonic designs of others. Third, at least in the near to mid term, the interests and objectives of China, Turkey, and Iran largely coincide with U.S. interests and objectives. These countries share a common interest with the United States in maintaining regional stability. Moreover, if successfully implemented, the policies of these three states would support the independence and sovereignty of the Caspian states, increase access to the region's oil and gas resources, and promote economic development and domestic stability. Thus, despite the preoccupation of many analysts with the rivalries and competition for influence among extraregional powers and the tendency to portray the "great game" in zero-sum terms, there are elements of open and tacit cooperation among these countries. Fourth, even if the intentions of these countries (and Russia) were to become more threatening in the long run, they would confront serious limits on their ability to project influence in a meaningful way. Finally, given the limited nature of U.S. interests in the region as well as the limits on American influence, the United States is likely to cooperate with these countries to maintain a favorable regional balance of power.

Chapter Five

TRANSNATIONAL THREATS

The spread of radical political Islam, the criminalization of state institutions and economic transactions, the increase in cross-border narcotics trafficking, and the potential proliferation of weapons of mass destruction (WMD) represent an interrelated network of transnational challenges to the states and societies within the Caspian region and serve as a potential catalyst for conflicts among these states and between the Caspian states and their neighbors.[1]   In addition, these transnational issues have the potential to challenge the security of the West.

Organized crime has the ability to corrupt and undermine the already weak institutions in many of these states. To the extent that organized crime takes over the functions of the state, particularly those of local law enforcement and the military, repression of society may increase. As these states become further weakened, they become more vulnerable to challenges from internal and external extremists, including radical political Islamic movements that feed on society's resentment and fear of chaos. This weakness, in turn, threatens to spill over into neighboring countries. The wars in Tajikistan, Chechnya, and Afghanistan have contributed to the

---

[1]See Graham Turbiville, "Flashpoints in Central Asia: Sources of Tension and Conflict—Drug and Weapons Trafficking," paper presented at the U.S. Institute of Peace, Washington, DC, May 16, 1997; and Nancy Lubin, "New Security Threats in the Southern Tier," in Rajan Menon, Yuri Fyodorov, and Ghia Nodia (eds.), *Russia, the Caucasus, and Central Asia: The 21st Century Security Environment*, M. E. Sharpe, Armonk, NY, June 1999.

emergence of political terrorism and the rise of Islamic extremism throughout the region.

The criminalization of the economy and the increase in political extremism and terrorism are also tied to the threat of WMD proliferation in Central Asia and the south Caucasus.[2] Although political leaders have pledged to work together to curb the smuggling in weapons and narcotics that has increased as borders have become more porous and enforcement more problematic, the task is beyond the capability of any of these states either individually or collectively. Although there is no hard evidence of the transport of fissile material or chemical/biological weapons (CBW) along the main smuggling routes, there is a growing concern that the logistical capability exists.[3] This capability presents a potentially critical challenge to both NATO and the West. The challenge is both direct, since the trade routes bring drugs and weapons to Russia and Europe, and indirect, because the rise in criminal trade and terrorism fuels conflicts between Caspian states attempting to preempt the spillover of these problems. This chapter examines the likelihood of both WMD proliferation and the spread of political Islam in this region and the implications of these trends for NATO and the West. The related issues of the increased trade in narcotics and the spread of organized crime are beyond the scope of this study and are discussed only as they have a bearing upon more traditional transnational geopolitical and security issues.[4]

---

[2]See "Hearings on International Organized Crime and Its Impact on the United States," Senate Hearing 103-899, Senate Permanent Subcommittee on Investigations, 103d Congress, 2nd Session, 1994.

[3]The main narcotics and weapons smuggling routes are believed to be the Khorog-Osh highway through Tajikistan's border with Afghanistan and across the mountains into the Fergana Valley in Kyrgyzstan, and the port city of Batumi in Georgia. See Irina Zviagelskaia and Vitalii Naumkin, "The Southern Tier: Non-Traditional Threats, Challenges and Risks for Russia's Security," in Rajan Menon, Yuri Fyodorov, and Ghia Nodia (eds.) (1999).

[4]The spread of organized crime and the drug trade and their implications for regional security have been the subject of several additional excellent studies including Graham H. Turbiville, Jr., *Mafia in Uniform, the Criminalization of the Russian Armed Forces*, Foreign Military Studies Office, July 1995; and Turbiville, "Narcotics Trafficking in Central Asia: A New Colombia," *Military Review*, Vol. LXXII, No. 12, December 1992, pp. 55–63.

THE RISK OF WMD PROLIFERATION[5]

Ever since the breakup of the Soviet Union, some policymakers and analysts have worried that parts of the former Soviet Union could contribute to the spread of weapons of mass destruction. The decisions by Ukraine, Belarus, and Kazakhstan, which inherited portions of the Soviet Union's nuclear arsenal at the time of independence, to become nonnuclear states and to sign the nuclear Non-Proliferation Treaty (NPT), eased much of this concern. So, too, did Russia's withdrawal of tactical nuclear weapons stockpiled on the territory of former republics. Nonetheless, some observers still worry that the combination of fragile and unstable states and multiple threats in the Caspian security environment could lead to the further spread of WMD.

NATO must worry about three types of WMD threats in the Caspian region: (1) countries could seek to acquire their own weapons of mass destruction; (2) these countries could become a direct or indirect source of proliferation of weapons grade material, technology, and expertise to other areas, either because of government policies or because governments lack the capability to control exports and borders; and (3) terrorist groups could acquire WMD, particularly chemical and biological weapons, for blackmail or regime destabilization.

A close examination of the factors that motivate countries to seek WMD suggests, as Figure 3 below indicates, that at least in the short-to-medium term, there is a minimal risk that the countries of Central Asia and the south Caucasus will seek to acquire WMD. In judging the risks of WMD acquisition, several factors need to be taken into account:

- Whether any states would seek a WMD capability for national security reasons, e.g., to deter WMD or conventional military threats by a hostile state

---

[5]The discussion of the WMD threat in the Caspian region is based on extensive interviews with U.S. government officials. The authors wish to express their gratitude to those individuals who agreed to be interviewed for this project. See also William C. Potter, *Nuclear Profiles of the Soviet Successor States*, Monterey Institute of International Studies, Monterey, CA, May 1993.

- Whether there are any powerful bureaucratic or political interests within these states that might seek a WMD capability for parochial reasons

- Whether any of the states might seek to acquire WMD for prestige or to establish their national identities or fulfill nationalist aspirations

- Whether the country has the resources and the technological wherewithal to develop and produce WMD

- How these countries weigh the benefits of WMD acquisition against the potential military, economic, and political costs and risks.

At least for the foreseeable future, countries in Central Asia and the south Caucasus probably will not seek a WMD capability, because of the following considerations:

- For most of these countries, security and defense against external threats are not a high priority. The current regimes see more

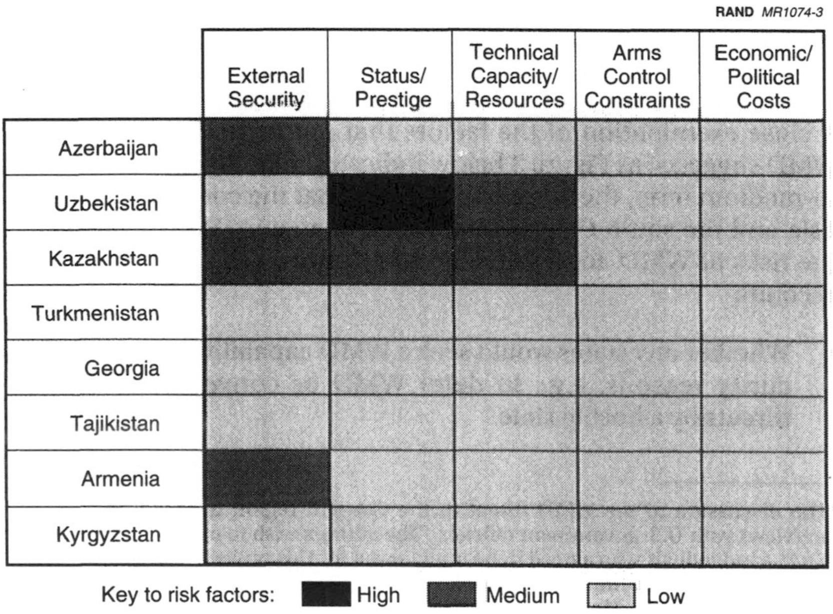

RAND MR1074-3

	External Security	Status/ Prestige	Technical Capacity/ Resources	Arms Control Constraints	Economic/ Political Costs
Azerbaijan	High	Low	Low	Low	Low
Uzbekistan	Low	High	High	Low	Low
Kazakhstan	High	High	High	Low	Low
Turkmenistan	Low	Low	Low	Low	Low
Georgia	Low	Low	Low	Low	Low
Tajikistan	Low	Low	Low	Low	Low
Armenia	Medium	Low	Low	Low	Low
Kyrgyzstan	Low	Low	Low	Low	Low

Key to risk factors: ■ High ■ Medium □ Low

Figure 3—The Risks of Proliferation

immediate threats to security arising from internal stability, for which WMD are irrelevant and possibly counterproductive. From the perspective of the ruling elites, WMD development would have a detrimental effect on economic development, which they see as key to their survival and to long-term political and social stability.

- Some of the neo-communist governments, notwithstanding their rhetoric, see Russia as the ultimate guarantor of security and the status quo, rather than a military or security threat. Development of WMD would put at risk the military cooperation, bilateral alliances, and collective defense arrangements that help maintain external security.

- Given their modest plans for force development, the militaries of the various countries are unlikely to pose a conventional military threat to any of their neighbors.

- Because of the Russian presence in Central Asian military and security establishments, it is unlikely that any country could covertly acquire or develop a WMD capability. The Russians would, therefore, be in a position to raise the costs of such a program, which would be a serious risk given the continued military and economic dependence of these countries on Russia.

- None of these countries has powerful nuclear establishments whose parochial interests would be served by developing WMD. With the exception of Kazakhstan and Uzbekistan, none of the states in the Caspian region has aspirations for regional leadership or domination that might be advanced by WMD possession.

- These countries do not possess any stocks of weapons grade or fissionable material and, because most were not part of the old Soviet nuclear weapons infrastructure, do not have a cadre of scientific, engineering, and technological expertise. Further, all nuclear weapons of the former Soviet Union have been removed from these countries.

- In general, none of the Caspian countries has the economic and technological means, at least in the near term, to develop WMD or the interest in allocating scarce resources to this task, which would retard economic development.

- Finally, all the countries of Central Asia and the south Caucasus are members of the NPT. Hence, any civilian nuclear reactors they might build would be subject to International Atomic Energy Agency (IAEA) safeguards. In addition, these countries are members of the Chemical Weapons Convention (CWC) and Biological Weapons Convention (BWC), which erect additional obligations to forgo CBW development.

Tajikistan

As the poorest and least successful of the Central Asian states, Tajikistan lacks the resources for a WMD program. Moreover, the current regime in Tajikistan is heavily dependent on Moscow (and others) for its survival and totally absorbed with managing its ethnic, tribal, regional, resource, and economic problems. Although Tajik officials fear Uzbek chauvinism and irredentism, they are likely to view the presence of WMD on their territory as a liability rather than an asset, in light of the potential for ethnic conflict and renewed civil strife.

Kyrgyzstan

Kyrgyzstan does not feel threatened by any external actors; instead, Bishkek's main security concerns are control of the country's porous borders and spillover of instability from Tajikistan. Accommodation with Russia is a central tenet of Kyrgyz security policy, and such a security orientation would be jeopardized by pursuit of a WMD capability. Moreover, Kyrgyzstan, like Tajikistan, lacks the resources to develop WMD and would be extremely vulnerable to outside pressure, isolation, and sanctions were it to pursue such an effort.

Turkmenistan

Turkmenistan does not see any external threat to its security. Indeed, President Niyazov has said that he could not foresee a threat to Turkmenistan for at least the next ten years.[6] While the government is continuing to evolve a distinct security doctrine, two central tenets

---

[6]See Bess A. Brown, "Security Concerns of the Central Asian States," in Jed C. Snyder (ed.) (1995), p. 80.

are already evident: first, Turkmenistan can best ensure its security and national self-identify through economic development; and, second, the country should avoid entanglements in alliances and collective security arrangements that could embroil it in the region's many conflicts.

Kazakhstan

In view of its decision to relinquish nuclear weapons and to join the NPT as a nonnuclear weapons state, it is difficult to envision circumstances under which Kazakhstan would decide to pursue a WMD capability. To be sure, many Kazakhs remain fearful and suspicious of Russia, and worry that Kazakhstan's security could be threatened by the revival of a neo-imperial or expansionist Russia. At the same time, however, Kazakhstan is more vulnerable to Russian pressure and more dependent on Russia's economic system than any other country in the region. Moreover, even though Kazakhstan developed a capable nuclear infrastructure during the Soviet days, many of its members were ethnic Russians who would be unlikely to cooperate with the Kazakh government in an effort to acquire WMD. Further, most Kazakhs have a strong "allergy" to nuclear weapons because of the ecological disaster caused by Soviet nuclear testing and weapons development in Kazakhstan. Thus, any decision by Kazakhstan to acquire nuclear or other unconventional weapons would be highly unpopular and potentially destabilizing.

Uzbekistan

Of all the countries in Central Asia, Uzbekistan probably represents the most plausible proliferation risk, but the odds that Tashkent would seek a WMD capability are nevertheless low, especially in the absence of any perception of a Russian or Chinese military threat. To be sure, Uzbekistan aspires to regional domination, is preoccupied with national status, and has the potential economic and technical resources to support a WMD program. Moreover, Uzbekistan has outstanding territorial and ethnic conflicts with Tajikistan and Kyrgyzstan, and fears the possible fragmentation of Afghanistan and the formation of a "greater Tajikistan." Faced with these threats to their territorial integrity and national unity, future Uzbek leaders might see WMD as the ultimate guarantor of security or as an instrument of coercion and intimidation in resolving its many disputes or pressing its irredentist claims. On the other hand, Uzbekistan would face formidable challenges to acquiring WMD: It has no known quantities of fissile material and no plans to build the necessary facilities to produce such material; like other Central Asian states, Uzbekistan is a member of the NPT, and thus any facilities it might build would be subject to IAEA and possibly supplemental bilateral safeguards; and Uzbek leaders have made it clear that they will continue to depend on Russia to guarantee Uzbek security and stability—a relationship that could be imperiled if the Uzbeks sought a truly independent defense identity based on possession of WMD.

Azerbaijan

The Azeris would appear to have neither the motives nor the means to acquire a WMD capability. Baku's priority is to develop relations with the West, and Azeri officials understand that such ties would be put in jeopardy by a WMD program. Although the Azeris have serious differences with Armenia and Iran and remain worried about Russia, they are unlikely to see WMD as an advantage in thwarting potential threats from these countries. Instead, Baku is allocating its resources to improving Azerbaijan's conventional, border control, and internal security forces to contain threats from Armenia and Iran, and is relying on its growing contacts with the West to counterbalance Russian power. Although profits from oil and gas exports could provide the resources to develop or acquire WMD, Azerbaijan has no WMD infrastructure, and its resources are likely to be used to address the country's more pressing economic and social problems and to improve its conventional defenses.

The Risk of Leakage

There appears to be little risk that the south Caucasus region could contribute to the leakage of WMD-related technology and materiel. The Soviet-era WMD infrastructure has disappeared, and the United States and local governments are cooperating in strengthening export control systems, border controls, and the security of sensitive WMD-related items.

There is virtually no Soviet-era infrastructure remaining in the south Caucasus. Basic research in advanced science in Georgia and Armenia was not directly part of weapons development. Armenia continues to plan for nuclear power production; however, the reactors are not configured for the production of weapons-grade material. Armenia's existing nuclear reactors, because of their poor maintenance and location in an earthquake zone, pose a safety rather than proliferation problem. Likewise, Azerbaijan poses no proliferation threat—its WMD infrastructure is virtually nonexistent and the Azeris have made strides in establishing more effective export and border controls as part of its broader strategy to improve relations with the West and attract foreign investment for oil-related and infrastructure projects. Although some chemical weapons (CW) depots for riot control agents probably remain on Azeri territory, these stocks are not usable because of safety problems. Finally, the danger that these countries could become transshipment points for the illicit transfer of nuclear material has receded somewhat, largely because of U.S. export control and border security assistance. Given the priority the U.S. government attaches to controlling WMD material in the former Soviet Union, strong congressional support for this program, and the benefits host countries accrue from U.S. assistance, the United States is likely to remain engaged in this area for some time.

The risk of WMD leakage from Central Asia is somewhat more complicated. Much of the area, particularly Kazakhstan and, to a lesser degree, Uzbekistan, played a supporting role in the old Soviet WMD infrastructure; nevertheless, the risks of proliferation are minimal and likely to diminish further in the face of aggressive U.S. government efforts to police sensitive facilities and assist local governments in safeguarding nuclear material.

Much of the region's Soviet nuclear weapons production infrastructure, which was concentrated in Kazakhstan at Semipalatinsk, has decayed. Both the technical expertise that ran the facilities and the highly enriched uranium (HEU) associated with the operation of test reactors have been repatriated to Russia. In addition, the United States, with the cooperation of the government of Kazakhstan, removed a large quantity of HEU. Kazakhstan continues to operate an experimental breeder reactor at Aktau, a facility that could be configured to produce plutonium suitable for weapons fabrication. Although this is a source of concern, especially because of proximity to the Iranian littoral, the proliferation danger at Aktau has been reduced for several reasons:

- The plutonium stockpile is being relocated to Semipalatinsk, where it will be more secure under IAEA safeguards with the installation of improved arrangements for protecting, controlling, and accounting for the material.

- U.S. personnel at Aktau have improved monitoring and surveillance of the facility.

- With U.S. assistance, Kazakhstan has made considerable progress in upgrading border controls, especially along the Caspian Sea approach.

The Soviets maintained a portion of their CBW program in the region, but little of it remains. According to press reports, the Soviet Union constructed a plant in Stepnogorsk in Kazakhstan for BW production; however, according to Jonathan Tucker, director of the Chemical and Biological Weapons Project at the Center for Non-Proliferation Studies, the facility did not actually engage in large-scale production and it is unclear whether BW were stockpiled at the site.[7] This portion of the facility is now defunct, and most of the equipment has been returned to Russia, destroyed, or rendered inoperable. The Kazakhs, with U.S. assistance, are converting the remaining facility to civilian use.

Uzbekistan was also part of the Soviet BW program, but much of the associated infrastructure has atrophied. The Uzbeks and Kazakhs jointly control an island in the Aral Sea that was used as a BW testing facility; however, there were no known stockpiles of BW agents on the island. According to press reports, the United States is providing assistance to Uzbekistan for the destruction of a former Soviet CBW production facility.

With respect to the other Central Asian states, Tajikistan and Kyrgyzstan mine substantial quantities of uranium ore, but have no capability for enrichment. Neither country operates nuclear reactors nor has any weapons expertise. Similarly, Turkmenistan has no

---

[7]"Russia Challenged to Disclose Status of BW," *The Washington Post*, February 26, 1998.

WMD-related infrastructure, material, or expertise. Border security in all three countries remains porous, but the lack of controls has most benefitted trafficking in drugs and conventional arms.

At the substate level, there are several real concerns about the acquisition and threatened use of weapons of mass destruction to further terrorist aims in the region. The judgment of experts considering substate groups with limited financial means is that the risk in descending order is chemical, biological, and nuclear weapons development and use.[8] Chemical and biological weapons are relatively easy for small substate groups to construct using dual-purpose equipment and materials, whereas acquiring fissile material, as previously noted, is significantly more difficult. However, the probability of terrorist use of WMD is limited in the face of regional and financial obstacles:

- Subnational groups face the same limitations as do states in obtaining weapons material. No indigenous stocks of nuclear, chemical, or biological weapons material exist in the region. Furthermore, the presence of Russian as well as international monitoring organizations greatly complicates the prospects for illicit acquisition.

- Terrorist groups need sponsors or significant sources of wealth to develop and produce WMD. As discussed earlier, the most logical sponsors of such groups, such as Iran or other Persian Gulf states, have little interest in destabilizing the region, even in the name of an Islamic revolution. That said, there is one group with potential resources that may have an interest in destabilization: Russian organized crime groups. This possibility should be monitored.

In sum, at least for the next five to ten years, the states and likely substate terrorist groups of the south Caucasus and Central Asia generally lack both the motivation and the means to become a significant WMD proliferation threat. Should unanticipated threats to national security emerge, governments are likely to rely on more traditional

---

[8]James E. Goodby, "Loose Nukes: Security Issues on the U.S.-Russian Agenda," an Arthur and Frank Payne Lecture, Institute for International Studies, Stanford University, April 10, 1997.

means of defense and deterrence, such as conventional military preparations, alliance formation, and the search for an external protector. Moreover, even if these states acquired WMD, it is unlikely that, with the exception of an Armenian WMD threat to Turkey, such weapons would pose a threat to NATO's security or the security of moderate, pro-Western countries in the region, as long as these regimes remain out of the hands of militant, anti-Western Islamists.

THE SPREAD OF POLITICAL ISLAM

In the immediate aftermath of independence, there was a pervasive fear in the region of the spread of Islamic fundamentalism. To a large extent, this anxiety reflected a mistaken perception that the civil war in Tajikistan was the result of an Islamist opposition movement that was incited and supported by Iranian religious propaganda and extensive Iranian military and financial assistance. Since the negotiation of a cease-fire in Tajikistan and the consolidation of a fragile governing coalition, fears of rampant Islamic fundamentalism have abated. Furthermore, as noted earlier, Iran's decision to pursue its interests in a pragmatic manner have lessened anxieties about the growth of Islamic radicalism.

Eight years after the Caspian and Central Asian states gained their independence, Islam has not yet emerged as the dominant political force in the region, even though religious activism is on the rise. However, as Graham Fuller has observed, over the long term, local conditions could make Central Asia ripe for the growth of anti-Western Islamic radicalism. First, in a time of rapid change and transition, Islam resonates with those elements of society in search of national identity. Second, fundamentalist Islam has appeal as a reformist force, seeking to advance the cause of democratization, human rights, and social justice. Thus, many of the oppressed and downtrodden people of Central Asia, suffering under the repressive rule of authoritarian regimes, see Islamist movements as progressive in character. Third, with the exception of Kyrgyzstan, the Central Asian countries are governed by ex-communist elites who can no longer rely on communist ideology or Soviet-era political structures for political control. Fourth, even though many Central Asian leaders have jumped on the nationalist bandwagon to garner popular support, the popularity and legitimacy that ruling elites enjoyed at the time of independence are declining, in large measure because governments have been unable to meet the basic needs and expectations of the populace. Fifth, Islam flourishes under conditions that are prevalent throughout the region: political repression, economic deprivation and declining living standards, suppression of Islamic political activity, and the lack of legitimate and organized political institutions for the expression of popular grievances.[9]

It is not surprising, therefore, that there has been a renewal of interest in Islam throughout the region, as manifested in the creation of thousands of new mosques, the opening of new schools for Islamic education and training, the emergence of a more independent and activist generation of Islamist leaders (especially in Tajikistan and parts of Uzbekistan), the growing observance of traditional Islamic religious and cultural practices, and the growing popularity of the Islamic Renaissance Party. Moreover, Islamic awareness and influence are likely to grow as Soviet-era restrictions on Islamic religious and political activities are dismantled. Nonetheless, it is important to note that Islam in Central Asia, as elsewhere, is not monolithic but instead has separate strands, which should not be confused with "fundamentalism." In addition, other cleavages in these societies will play a role in shaping national identities and social mobilization.[10]

Thus, few would disagree with the observation of one expert that:

> No doubt, given that Islam is a vital part of their cultural makeup and the fact that for 70 years they were deprived of expressing their Islamic sentiments, Islam is bound to play a more prominent role in the social and political life of the ex-Soviet Muslim states as they begin to assert their cultural identity.[11]

In terms of Western security interests, however, what matters is not whether Islamic influence and awareness grow in Central Asia, but rather the *brand* of Islam that might emerge. A benign possibility is a

---

[9]See Graham E. Fuller (April 1994).

[10]See Rajan Menon, "After Empire: Russia and the Southern Near Abroad," in Michael Mandelbaum (ed.) (1998), p. 153.

[11]Shireen T. Hunter, "The Muslim Republics of the Former Soviet Union: Policy Challenges for the United States," *The Washington Quarterly*, Summer 1992, p. 57.

more moderate, secular, nontheocratic version based on the Turkish model. If this were to happen, the West would have little to fear from the revival of Islam in Central Asia. The more menacing prospect is that the region could be swept by a radical, revolutionary Islamic movement under Iran's influence and implacably hostile to Western interests in the greater Middle East and beyond. How likely is this threat and, if it is a serious risk, what options would NATO have to contain the expansion of Islamic radicalism and Iranian influence?

Although the influence of Islam and Islamic opposition groups is likely to grow, several factors militate against the emergence of militant, anti-Western Islamic governments and the formation of an Iranian-led pan-Islamic bloc:[12]

- Virtually all of Central Asia's Muslims (the main exception is Azerbaijan) are not Shia but Sunni, and from the conservative Hanafi sect. The predominant Sunni character of the Muslim republics makes them less receptive to Iranian influence. Additionally, Islam never sank deep roots throughout the less-urbanized parts of the region. In Kazakhstan, Turkmenistan, and Kyrgyzstan, in particular, the dominant nomadic culture was fallow ground for the growth of Islam.

- The countries of Central Asia do not harbor the anti-Western, anti-colonial sentiments that are the signature of the militant, radical Islamic movement, for several reasons. First, the growth of radical Islam in Iran and throughout the Arab world resulted from the failure of previous secular and Western-oriented governments to meet the political, economic, and social needs of their people. The popular disenchantment with these governments and the pervasive Western presence in the Arab world sparked the development of a militant, anti-Western Islamic orthodoxy there. These conditions do not exist in Central Asia: no country in the region has experimented with Western-style government or endured colonial or other forms of repressive Western rule. Second, much of radical Islam's anti-Western sentiment stems from the perception that the United States—and the West, in general—are biased toward Israel and hostile toward

---

[12]This discussion draws heavily on Shireen Hunter (1992).

Muslims. In contrast, the Muslim republics of Central Asia are essentially indifferent to the Arab-Israeli conflict—indeed some have forged close ties with Israel—and thus Western support for Israel does not engender Central Asian resentment of the West.

- Most of the Islamic groups in Central Asia have yet to develop close ties with the Iranian clerical establishment and have not received significant financial or religious support from Tehran. As a result, Iran's ruling Islamic clergy exerts little influence over their co-religionists in Central Asia. Moreover, the leaders of Islamic groups in Central Asia have shown almost no interest in emulating the Iranian model.

Weighing the factors that might encourage the growth of radical Islam and the constraints on its development, it seems reasonable to conclude that the threat of Islamic fundamentalism has been exaggerated. As one scholar puts it:

> Thus, even if [the governments of the Muslim republics] were to adopt a social and political system based on Islam, it is unlikely that the newly independent Muslim states would display the sort of anti-Western sentiments observed among groups in the Middle East. Moreover, there is a significant difference between, on the one hand, desiring a more prominent place for Islam and Islamic culture in the society . . . and, on the other, desiring to establish a government and polity based on a militant and extremist interpretation of Islam.[13]

To say that it is unlikely that militant Islam will spread through the region is not to say it cannot happen. Government policies and practices—particularly how governments manage the wealth produced by a booming energy sector—will be key factors in determining the growth of Islamic fundamentalism. In general, if the leaders of the Caspian countries satisfy the rising political, economic, and social expectations of their populations, respect the rights of minorities and the rule of law, and move toward pluralistic and democratic forms of government, it will be difficult for extremist ideologies to take root.

---

[13]Hunter (1992).

There is no guarantee, however, that the leaders of the states in Central Asia and the south Caucasus will embrace democratic values or that energy-driven profits will promote domestic stability. On the contrary, there are signs that the leaders of Kazakhstan, Uzbekistan, and Turkmenistan seek to suppress political movements that could express political, cultural, and economic grievances in a legitimate and peaceful manner. The real question, therefore, is whether the states will provide good and effective governance. If the neo-communist leaders of Central Asia fail this test, the Islamist message—a call for democracy, human rights, social justice, better social services, Islamic values, and an end to corruption and privilege—will find fertile ground. And Islamic movements, whether indigenous or imported, are the prime candidates for opposition to the state, especially when the state suppresses other political parties as well. The greater the state repression, the more radical and violent Islamic movements generally are likely to become.   Militant crackdowns against any expression of Islam the state cannot control could lead to the creation of extremely violent, radicalized Islamic movements akin to those in Algeria and Egypt. In short, bad governance creates radical Islam, whether or not Iran is involved. And when wrapped in the mantle of nationalism, these radical Islamic movements could provide a rallying point for all disaffected elements of society.

Moreover, as a growing number of scholars and economists warn, experience has shown that resource wealth tends to have a negative effect on economic growth and, in the case of the Caspian states, could impede market reforms and exacerbate corruption that has reached near-epidemic proportions. The combination of growing economic inequality, runaway corruption, and exploding popular expectations of general prosperity is a potential recipe for violence and extremism.[14]

But even if events go sour and militant Islamic fundamentalism emerges as a serious political movement, it is unlikely that NATO would have a military role to play in containing or rolling back the growth of radical Islam, or even much leverage in trying to shape de-

---

[14]Ruseckas (1998), pp. 16–17.

velopments in a favorable manner through dialogue and consultation:

- Barring the emergence of fundamentalist rogue states that pose a WMD or conventional military threat to NATO members or key pro-Western governments in the Persian Gulf region, the odds are extremely low that NATO would want to undertake operations aimed at containing the spread of Islam in Central Asia.

- Other countries whose security would be directly threatened by radical Islam and who have greater capabilities to bring decisive influence to bear (most especially Russia) will defend their "special rights" to deal with this challenge and are unlikely to support a prominent role for NATO.

- The fortunes of radical Islam will be determined primarily by the internal dynamics of the Central Asian countries themselves; NATO's influence over this process is sharply limited and would almost certainly not be decisive.

In sum, military force is an inappropriate tool for containing the spread of radical Islam. The most effective way to deal with this potential danger, as many commentators have noted, is Western assistance for implementing programs that support free-market economic development, the rule of law and basic human rights, and the promotion of democratic and civic societies.[15]

---

[15]See, for example, Ariel Cohen, *The New Great Game: Oil Politics in the Caucasus and Central Asia* (1996).

Chapter Six

CASPIAN OIL AND ENERGY SECURITY

The vast and largely unexplored energy resources of the Caspian region present new opportunities for world oil markets, the region, and the United States:[1]

- The emergence of energy supplies would diversify world oil supplies and help restrain price increases during an expected period of rapidly growing demand for global oil. Significant quantities of Caspian oil exports would ease pressure on Persian Gulf production capacity and provide a hedge against oil supply disruptions.

- If well managed (and this is a big if), profits from oil and gas exports could stimulate economic growth and a rise in living standards in the energy-producing states, and thus alleviate many of the conditions that are a source of tension and instability. At today's market prices, the potential oil reserves of the Caspian Sea zone have an estimated value of between $2–$4 trillion. The availability of Caspian energy supplies on world markets will likewise enhance prospects for economic growth and political stability in key countries surrounding the region.

---

[1]Data on Caspian energy production and exports have been compiled from multiple sources. Choosing among the numerous and often divergent estimates of Caspian energy potential is fraught with difficulties. Our figures are derived primarily from the U.S. Department of Energy's *International Energy Outlook* (1997) and data cited in secondary sources. The most reliable and accurate of these are cited in Ruseckas (1998), fns. 6, 10.

- There are tremendous commercial opportunities for U.S. and Western multinational oil companies in Caspian Sea oil development and, more generally, in the development of the region's mineral resources and manufacturing and agricultural sectors. Today, over a dozen companies (mainly Western) have invested over $40 billion in the states of the region.[2] Under optimistic assumptions, the potential income for U.S.-dominated multinational oil companies could reach as high as $5–$10 billion annually by 2010. Chevroil alone is projecting a total profit of $20 billion from its investment in Kazakhstan. It is expected that the major oil-producing fields in Azerbaijan will yield profits of $50 billion or more at current prices.

The long-term outlook for global oil demand and supply underscores the potential significance of Caspian oil. According to the U.S. Energy Information Administration (EIA), current global demand for oil is around 72 million barrels per day (mb/d) and is expected to increase to about 103 mb/d by the year 2015.[3] Total natural gas consumption is currently around 78 trillion cubic feet (TCF) a year and natural gas could be used more heavily in the future instead of oil to meet new energy requirements in Europe and Asia, especially since there is a worldwide surplus of gas production capacity.

The lion's share of the increased demand for oil will be met by producers in the Persian Gulf. However, Caspian Sea oil could help meet these burgeoning energy needs. According to the U.S. government, the region has proven reserves of roughly 16 billion (bn) barrels of oil, which puts it roughly on a par with North Sea oil (see Figures 4 and 5).[4] Some estimates of the region's *potential* oil reserves range from 70 to 200 bn barrels, although most internal estimates of oil and gas industry analysts put the figure at 40 to 75 bn barrels, roughly comparable to North Sea reserves or, at best, Iraq's poten-

---

[2]This figure is quoted in S. Frederick Starr, "U.S. Interests in the Central Asian Republics," testimony delivered to the House Committee on International Relations (Subcommittee on Asia and the Pacific), February 12, 1998, pp. 1–2.

[3]Patrick Clawson, "Energy Security in a Time of Plenty," Strategic Forum Paper No. 130, NDU Press, Washington, DC, 1997, p. 3.

[4]Clawson (1997). Some estimates of proven oil reserves for the region range as high as 15 billion to 31 billion barrels.

tial.[5] Estimates of the area's proven and probable gas reserves range from 230–360 trillion TCF—as much as the combined reserves of the United States and Mexico, or about 7 percent of total world proven gas reserves.[6] According to the International Energy Agency forecast, oil exports from the Caspian Basin could reach 1.5 mb/d by early in the next century; under optimistic circumstances the region could export close to 2.3 mb/d by 2010, and thus meet about 7 percent of incremental growth in worldwide oil during this timeframe. In short, under any scenario, the Caspian could improve global energy security at the margins.

RAND *MR1074-4*

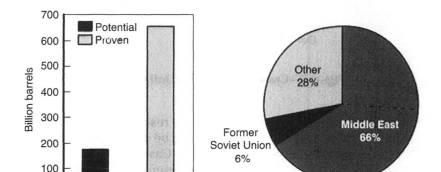

Total proven and potential oil reserves   Percentage of world's proven oil resources

Figure 4—Caspian Region Oil Outlook

---

[5]Ruseckas (1998), p. 4. There is much geological uncertainty surrounding estimates of possible oil reserves, and categorical projections should be treated with a grain of salt. Most estimates, however, fall within the 50–160 billion barrel range.

[6]See Ann Myers Jaffe, "Unlocking the Assets: Energy and the Future of Central Asia and the Caucasus," paper prepared for the James A. Baker III Institute for Public Policy, Rice University, April 1998.

RAND *MR1074-5*

Total proven and potential gas reserves

Percentage of world's proven gas resources

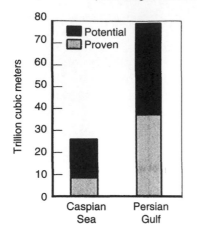

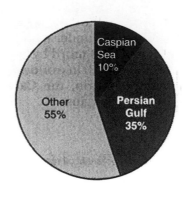

Figure 5—Caspian Region Gas Outlook

That said, the importance of Caspian energy resources to global energy supplies and energy security should not be overstated. In comparison to the global energy resource base, Caspian oil and gas reserves, as shown in Figures 4 and 5, represent a tiny fraction of overall supplies. Total proven reserves in the Caspian represent only 2.0 percent of total world proven oil reserves—one quarter of Venezuela's, one-seventh of Iraq's, and one-seventeenth of Saudi Arabia's (see Figure 4). Even if the region reached its maximum oil production potential, by the year 2010, exports would account for slightly less than 3 percent of global oil consumption (see Figure 6).[7]

Moreover, the degree to which the Caspian region's potential reserves are recovered and exported over the next 10–15 years remains uncertain.[8] Caspian oil will be expensive and technologically diffi-

---

[7]Jaffe (1998), p. 1.

[8]The following discussion draws heavily on Rosemarie Forsythe, *The Politics of Oil in the Caucasus and Central Asia*, Adelphi Paper 300, Oxford University Press for IISS, Oxford, 1996. Forsythe was one of the first observers to detail the many difficulties the

RAND *MR1074-6*

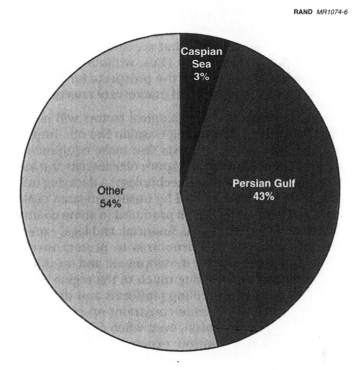

Figure 6—Caspian Oil Exports as a Percentage of Global Oil
Consumption: 2010

cult to find and develop. Indeed, there are numerous obstacles that
must bo overcome if these countries are to transport their oil and gas
to market. The most significant of these constraints include:

- **Geography.** There is no easy way to export energy from the
  Caspian Basin. The major energy-producing countries are land-
  locked and thus must rely on the cooperation of neighboring
  countries to ship their energy to market. Many of the potential

---

Caspian states face in bringing their oil and gas to market. Others have echoed this
sobering view. See, in particular, John Roberts, *Caspian Pipelines*, Royal Institute of
International Affairs, London, 1996, and Robert E. Ebel, *Energy Choices in the Near
Abroad: The Haves and the Have-Nots Face the Future*, The Center for Strategic and
International Studies, Washington, DC, April 1997.

pipeline routes pass through highly unstable and conflict-prone regions, such as Afghanistan and parts of the Caucasus and Turkey, or countries like Iran that are unreliable or undesirable partners for political reasons. Thus, without a diversified network of reliable access routes, the prospects for moving the oil from the ground to international markets are uncertain.

- **Technical Constraints.** Technological factors will increase the cost and difficulty of developing Caspian Sea oil. Impediments include high transportation costs that make equipment expensive to import and oil costly to export; obsolescent and inefficient oil exploration equipment and technology; a decaying infrastructure; oil fields heavily damaged by unsophisticated exploitation methods; the poor quality of oil produced in some countries; the lack of indigenous commercial, financial, and legal expertise; the absence of effective legal structures to protect investments, which discourages capital for development; and the difficult geological conditions surrounding much of the region's resources. The shortage of modern drilling platforms and drilling support material is an especially acute constraint on rapid exploration and development.[9] As a result, even when production increases, operating and transportation expenses for Caspian oil will be substantially higher than the same costs in other major oil-producing regions.

- **Political Problems.** Political developments within the region could pose barriers to oil development and export, including internal instability within oil-producing countries; administrative disorganization, mismanagement, and corruption; and Russian interventionism or obstructionism.

- **Capital.** Although oil and gas companies are lining up to secure lucrative contracts, it remains to be seen how much exploration, recovery, production, and transportation they will be able to finance with their own resources or in international capital markets. According to Cambridge Energy Research Associates, it will take $70–$100 billion to develop and transport the region's oil reserves and roughly the same amount to develop its gas re-

---

[9]See Jaffe (1998).

serves.[10] In particular, the availability of financing for very expensive pipeline construction projects, such as the proposed Baku-Ceyhan pipeline, is questionable.[11] Although, in theory, the major international capital markets could provide assistance, many multinational companies may seek higher returns on capital investments elsewhere (e.g., by opening new fields in Saudi Arabia), and may be further inhibited by the political and economic risks associated with oil exploitation and export as well as rampant corruption and administrative mismanagement. The recent turmoil in Asian financial markets and the general uneasiness about investing in emerging markets may also discourage capitalization of Caspian energy projects.

- **Legal Problems.** Continuing disputes over conflicting territorial claims, as well as lack of protection for private property rights, are also roadblocks to oil production and distribution in that they create uncertainty about ownership of investments and oil resources. In addition to the unresolved issue of Caspian sea boundaries, there are outstanding questions concerning the legal status of the Bosporus Straits that cloud access to the most viable route for Caspian Sea oil to reach the Mediterranean and world markets.

Furthermore, as Patrick Clawson has observed, other trends affecting the global oil outlook could also work against a significant role for Caspian Sea oil.[12] First, world demand for oil could grow less rapidly than forecasted. For example, world economic growth could slow down, concern over global warming could lead to new restrictions on fuel consumption, subsidies for energy consumption in the developing world could be reduced, energy-inefficient state-owned industries in China and Russia could be modernized or closed, and natural

---

[10]As cited in Zanny Minton-Beddoes, "A Caspian Gamble," *The Economist,* February 7, 1998, p. 6 of insert.

[11]Prospects have dimmed recently for the construction of a main export pipeline that would carry the bulk of Azeri long-term oil to the Turkish Mediterranean port of Ceyhan. The estimated cost of $4 billion was a major factor in the decision to delay the project, along with low crude oil prices and disappointing results from ongoing drilling operations in Azerbaijan that have led some oil company analysts to question the size of the region's recoverable reserves.

[12]See Clawson (1998) for an excellent treatment of trends in the international oil market, which is summarized here.

gas could be substituted for oil. Because of the high costs of Caspian oil production, slack world demand for oil and low or declining oil prices would make Caspian oil exploitation less commercially attractive. Indeed, it is estimated that the cost to produce a barrel of Caspian oil will be three to five times higher than that of other low-cost producing areas.

Second, over the past decade, there has been a substantial increase in the supply of oil from sources both within and outside of the Organization of Petroleum Exporting Countries (OPEC)—resulting mainly from lower production costs and the removal of restrictions impeding production—and the prospects for ample oil supplies, excluding Caspian Sea oil, are good for the foreseeable future. In the last decade, 13 non-OPEC countries increased their combined production by over 2.0 mb/d, and U.S. oil output is expected to increase for at least the next five years. Additionally, many Middle Eastern oil producers are poised to increase production capacity substantially, which is technically feasible given their ample oil reserves. Notwithstanding its recent decision to cut·oil production, which was driven largely by short-term considerations, Saudi Arabia has long-term plans to increase its capacity by 3 mb/d (from 11 mb/d to 14 mb/d); other Gulf Arab oil-producing states are increasing their capacity by 2 mb/d, and both Iraq and Iran are producing well below their maximum capacity—a situation that is likely to change over the next 10 to 15 years. Furthermore, substantial reserves remain to be exploited in Africa, South America, and offshore Asia. Finally, the long-term possibility cannot be ruled out that Russia might reverse its decline in oil production and increase its output. On the margins, increasing oil production in any of these countries would be quicker, more profitable, and less difficult than an equivalent increase in Caspian oil production. Non-OPEC oil production has increased by 1 to 1.5 percent per annum, on average, since 1988. If this trend continues, and assuming continuing competition within OPEC, access to increased Caspian oil exports will have little or no effect in moderating oil price increases.

From the West and NATO's perspective, therefore, while the emergence of the Caspian Sea region as an important source of global energy will contribute to improved energy security, Caspian energy supplies are unlikely to become critical to the West's security and prosperity, or a potential strategic vulnerability. Even under the most optimistic scenario, the role of Caspian energy supplies in world oil markets will be overshadowed by the Persian Gulf. Moreover, it is unlikely that the region will realize its full potential for some time (if at all), given the constraints on rapid oil development and other factors that are likely to create an oversupply of oil for the next decade, even if the demand for it is high. Consequently, it is highly unlikely that the world will become heavily dependent on Caspian energy. Second, any severe interruption in the flow of Caspian oil is unlikely to cause more than a temporary dislocation in the availability of oil on the world market and a modest increase in prices. There are several reasons for this prognosis:

- Any short-term disruption in Caspian oil supplies would trigger an increase in oil prices; at these higher prices, some wells that have been capped temporarily for commercial reasons would be reopened. Though there would almost certainly be a lag time, the long-term availability of this oil would calm the market and cushion the long-term effects of an interruption in Caspian Sea oil. Saudi Arabia, in particular, has the technical capacity to bring additional oil on-line fairly quickly and at a relatively low cost. Other oil supplies from outside the Persian Gulf would also be available to offset the loss of Caspian oil.

- Even under the most optimistic conditions, the world will likely import only a tiny fraction of its energy requirements from the Caspian Sea region. By the year 2010, world demand for oil is expected to reach roughly 100 m/bd. Almost half (14 mb/d) of the projected increase in the global demand for oil in 2010 will come from east Asia (excluding Indonesia and India). By contrast, demand in the advanced industrial nations of Europe and North America is projected to grow only 6 mb/d. According to one estimate, crude oil imports from the Asia-Pacific region are projected to increase from 58 percent to 72 percent over the next seven years, and by 2010, it is estimated that this region, with China and India in the forefront, will consume 18 mb/d of Persian Gulf oil, or more than Europe and the United States combined.[13]

---

[13]See Geoffrey Kemp and Robert E. Harkavy, *The Strategic Geography of the Changing Middle East,* Carnegie Endowment for International Peace, Washington, DC, May 1997, p. 120.

- As noted earlier, even if all the obstacles to Caspian Sea oil devel-opment were overcome, the region would account for a tiny por-tion of global oil production. Moreover, oil reserves in the Caspian Sea put the region on a par with oil from the North Sea or Iraq. For the past seven years, only a trickle of oil has been ex-ported from Iraq, yet the international oil market has adjusted quite well to this decline. Even if the growth in world demand for oil should exceed expectations, there is likely to be considerable spare or underutilized capacity in the Persian Gulf—and perhaps Russia—that could be brought on-line fairly quickly.

- Depending on the degree of diversification of oil export outlets in the region, a total interruption of oil supplies appears highly un-likely. Even under the most pessimistic assumptions, there will probably be at least two main pipelines for long-term exports of Caspian oil. If this degree of redundancy is achieved, it is hard to imagine the spigot going completely dry.

To be sure, given the range of uncertainties surrounding projections of global oil demand and supply, it is possible that the above projec-tions could be off target. Under a worst-case scenario, world de-mand for oil could greatly exceed production; excess capacity both within and outside the Persian Gulf region could dry up; Caspian Sea oil exports could reach their maximum potential; and the one or two pipelines carrying Caspian Sea oil to market would be highly vulner-able to interdiction.

Under these gloomy assumptions, the West—and especially Turkey—could be hard hit by a prolonged interruption in Caspian Sea oil supplies. If the disruption were caused by a state or states that controlled pipelines, NATO or some coalition of Western coun-tries would have the option of bringing military pressure to bear to coerce the state into resuming the flow of oil. For this option to be credible, Turkey's cooperation would be required, because of its proximity to the region and the difficulty NATO would have in pro-jecting conventional forces into the region without access to Turkish bases. Even with full Turkish cooperation, however, the coercive use of force to compel a country to resume oil exports would be highly controversial, especially if the country were Russia, and it is uncer-tain at best that NATO would agree to such an undertaking or that the United States could assemble an effective ad hoc coalition for such a purpose. Indeed, under these circumstances, the impulse of most countries would likely be to tolerate dislocations arising from higher oil prices rather than incur the political, resource, and military costs associated with the use of force to restore oil exports from the Caspian.[14]

An interdiction of Caspian Sea oil supplies resulting from terrorist or subnational attacks on oil pipelines and the associated infrastructure would pose a more difficult challenge to NATO. As most studies have shown, pipeline distribution systems are highly vulnerable to attack, even though the damage often can be quickly repaired. If the pipeline is above ground, portions of it can be blown up using a variety of low-tech methods; if the pipeline is buried, it is nonetheless vulnerable at its exposed and usually undefended pumping stations, input terminals, river crossings, and intersystem linkings. For instance, any one of the over 100 points on the Trans-Arabian pipeline could, if damaged or destroyed, halt product movement. Destroying pumping stations may cripple the use of a pipeline for up to six months. Also vulnerable to attack are the centralized, computerized control of pipeline systems that enables valves to be opened or closed and pumps to be started or stopped remotely. Natural gas pipelines are especially vulnerable to interdiction because they must maintain a constant flow of pressure. In short, even under a worst-case scenario, it is far from clear that NATO's use of military force would be appropriate or effective. Equally problematical is whether NATO could reach consensus on a decision to use force in such circumstances.

Finally, there are other factors to bear in mind. First, until recently there was no Western access to Caspian oil supplies. Throughout the Cold War, this situation was of no strategic consequence to the West, and trends in the global oil market over the next 10–15 years will not alter this reality.

Second, the world economy needs to ensure the availability of oil to the global market. Because oil is a global commodity that is traded on an international market, the West benefits from the delivery of oil to any market, regardless of the source or the buyer, unless there are

---

[14]This is also the judgment of Martha Brill Olcott (Summer 1998), p. 111.

true oil shortages, which is clearly not the case for the foreseeable future.

Third, physical possession of oil wells is no longer a vital concern; thus, fear that Caspian oil could "fall into the wrong hands" is a slogan of dubious value, since much of the world's energy is already in the "wrong hands" and yet is of little consequence. Qaddafi, Saddam, and the Ayatollahs of Iran have never hesitated to sell oil to the West, in as much quantity as we want. Even in the unlikely event that Russia established control over all Caspian oil, it would hardly matter, either economically or geopolitically, because even Russia will sell this oil.

Notwithstanding much of the hyperbole that surrounds what has been written about Caspian oil, it is hard to escape the conclusion that the energy potential of the Caspian basin is of limited geostrategic significance. As two prominent experts on the region have noted, the global strategic significance of the Caspian region with respect to energy resources pales in comparison to that of the Persian Gulf. Indeed, based on most reliable estimates, including those of the EIA, by the year 2010, Persian Gulf oil exports will amount to 40–45 mb/d, a little under half of the world's total requirements. Hence, there is no realistic alternative to Persian Gulf oil supplies to meet the growing demand during this period.[15]

In sum, the treatment of energy security in the Caspian, which mirrors in general the discussion in the academic literature, has become oversimplified and sloganized. Western access to Caspian oil is not strategically significant. Rather, the West has a modest stake in helping to ensure that (1) conflict in the region does not impede the flow of oil, (2) no truly hostile state has a huge monopoly over oil, (3) U.S. and Western companies have a shot at the profits from oil development, and (4) no state has a monopoly over regional pipelines. Overall, these are important, but hardly vital, interests.

---

[15]Kemp and Harkavy (1997), p. 111.

Chapter Seven

IMPLICATIONS FOR NATO AND WESTERN POLICY AND PLANNING

The south Caucasus and Central Asia will be of growing geopolitical significance to the West and NATO over the next 10–15 years because of their potential contribution to global energy supplies and energy security and the risk that conflict and instability could spread beyond the region, invite foreign military intervention, provoke a resurgence of Russian neo-imperialism, redefine the territorial status quo, and alter geopolitical relationships among several major powers.

Given these stakes, the West will need to increase and sustain its engagement and fashion a comprehensive long-term strategy aimed at promoting democratic and economic development and helping to alleviate the root causes of conflict and instability. The key political, economic, and diplomatic components of a coherent Western security strategy should include:[1]

- Periodic high-level statements by Western governments affirming the importance they attach to the development of independent, secure, stable free-market democracies in the Caspian region.

---

[1] For sound prescriptions for Western policy toward the region, which are synthesized in the recommendations below, see Ariel Cohen, U.S. *Policy in the Caucasus and Central Asia: Building a New "Silk Road" to Economic Prosperity*, The Heritage Foundation, Backgrounder No. 1132, Washington, DC, July 29, 1997; F. Stephen Larrabee (1997), pp. 171–173; and Rajan Menon, "Central Asia's Foreign Policy and Security Challenges: Implications for the United States," *National Bureau of Asian Research Analysis*, Vol. 6, No. 4, December 1995, pp. 13–15.

- Strong U.S. and European support for multiple pipelines for the transit of Caspian oil and gas supplies.

- U.S. encouragement of the EU and international institutions such as the World Bank and the European Bank for Reconstruction and Development (EBRD) to become more actively engaged in developing the region's oil and gas supplies, especially its infrastructure, legal framework, and technical expertise.

- An expansion of Western support for programs and activities to promote democracy and market reforms; respect for rights of minorities; improved social and economic conditions, market institutions, and the rule of law; and functioning legal systems. Much of this work can be done through nongovernmental organizations.

- Increased Western economic and technical assistance to states in the region to improve their capabilities to cope with transnational challenges, including aid to combat illegal drug trafficking and arms trade, strengthen border and export controls, manage refugee problems, respond to natural disasters, and repair ecological/environmental damage.

- Stronger U.S. and European support for OSCE initiatives to prevent and resolve ethnic and regional conflicts in the south Caucasus and Central Asia.

- Greater Western support for expanding the role of the OSCE and UN in the region, especially in monitoring human rights and the media, assisting in economic legislation, facilitating the return of refugees and the delivery of humanitarian assistance, and assistance with family planning and health care programs.[2]

- The formation of a "contact group," perhaps under the OSCE's umbrella, to begin a dialogue on energy security issues. This group might be made up of those countries with the strongest stake in ensuring access to the region's energy supplies.[3]

---

[2]On the potential contribution of the OSCE to regional security and stability, see Bruce George, "NATO, OSCE, and Regional Security Issues in Central Asia and the Caucasus," *Perceptions*, December 1997–February 1998, p. 139.

[3]George (1998), p. 141.

- Continued Western support for those forces in Russia (e.g., oil and gas companies) that favor cooperation with the West in the development of the region's energy resources. The most effective means for securing this cooperation is to support Russian participation in Caspian energy development and pipeline construction.[4]

- Greater Western aid and investment in the development of Central Asian regional economic and security structures.

- Increased Western support for cooperative arrangements among the country's extraregional powers (e.g., Iran, Turkey, Pakistan) to promote economic integration.

A viable and sustainable Western security strategy for the region must be based on a sound understanding of the nature of NATO's security interests both in the region and vis-à-vis Russia, the risk to those interests, and the capabilities NATO can bring to bear to shape a favorable security environment. What role should NATO play in responding to the emerging dangers and opportunities in the Caspian security environment? What are the implications of security trends for NATO's commitments, force planning, and military requirements and activities? What peacetime activities could NATO undertake to shape an environment that would prevent threats to Western interests from emerging? Is there a role here for NATO in crisis management and peacekeeping? Should NATO consider new security tasks or Article V–type commitments for the region?

In answering these questions and designing an overall strategy, NATO should be guided by several fundamental considerations:

- First, over the next decade, Western interests in the Caspian Zone will be best protected by political, economic, and energy measures to promote stability, market economies, and democracy and to reduce the dependence of the Caspian states on Russia.

- Second, the greatest threats to the security and stability of the Caspian states are internal. Western policy should, therefore, fo-

---

[4]See statement by Rep. Lee Hamilton (D-Ind.), as cited in the *Journal of Commerce*, July 14, 1998.

cus on resolving the political, economic, and social challenges that could breed internal conflict and instability.

- Third, the United States and other NATO militaries can help the Caspian states to reform and restructure their armed forces, which would in turn help stabilize these countries and consolidate democratic reforms. These goals can be accomplished with training and advisory assistance. Such assistance could be conditioned on progress individual Caspian countries make toward implementing serious democratic and economic reforms. NATO's combat capabilities, on the other hand, are simply not relevant to the major challenges confronting these countries.

- Fourth, U.S., Western, and NATO resources and leverage are limited. Therefore, Western objectives should be fairly modest to avoid a potentially dangerous gap between capabilities and commitments.

- Fifth, Russia is likely to remain an influential and, in some cases, the predominant power in the region for some time. Thus, its legitimate interest in security and stability along its borders should be accommodated. But Russia should recognize that the establishment of stable, prosperous, and independent states along its periphery is in its interests. Consequently, NATO advice and training to local militaries, if attuned to Russian sensibilities, need not work at cross-purposes with a strategy of engaging Russia on matters of concern to the West.

- Sixth, as Rajan Menon has argued, given America's existing commitments in other parts of the world and NATO's other priorities, the Alliance should avoid creating expectations among the Caspian states that NATO's interests in the region are so important that it will keep them secure from Russia. NATO is not likely to be willing to deliver on any such promise, and "raising such false hopes will not merely breed disillusionment . . . but could be downright destabilizing if it encourages Russia's neighbors to take steps based on an understanding of American policy that turns out to be incorrect."[5]

---

[5]Menon (February 1998), p. 36.

PEACETIME MILITARY ACTIVITIES

Many of the Caspian states are interested in developing and expanding military contacts with NATO and in enhancing their participation in the Alliance's PfP program. Developing closer military relations between NATO and the Caspian states offers several benefits. Enhanced training and military-to-military contacts, for example, demonstrate Western interest, bolster the independence of the Caspian states, and promote regional cooperation. Increasing the frequency and scope of peacekeeping exercises under the PfP program would contribute to these objectives.

At the same time, many European members of NATO are reluctant to deepen their military engagement in the former Soviet Union, as evidenced by their tepid support for CENTRASBAT. The Russians, moreover, are deeply suspicious of these activities, which have prompted growing claims in some quarters that NATO is seeking to establish military control over the region. Further, there is a danger that deepening NATO's ties with the Caspian states will raise false expectations about the Alliance's commitment to their security. For all these reasons, therefore, NATO should proceed gradually in expanding military relations with the Caspian states. Should NATO decide to forge ahead with military cooperation with local states, the Alliance should, to the extent feasible, seek to allay Russia's anxieties by involving the Russians more closely in the planning and implementation of these activities. Additionally, increased U.S./NATO transparency about these programs might lessen the risk of a negative Russian reaction.

While NATO's role in encouraging peacetime military cooperation with the Caspian states is necessarily limited, the United States faces fewer such obstacles and may have a larger role. In fact, given the very real dangers of instability in a region that may involve U.S. and Western security interests and objectives, the United States Air Force (USAF) may be asked to increase its presence there. The U. S. Department of Defense has already made significant commitments, most recently to both Azerbaijan and Georgia. Secretary Cohen announced in March 1998 that American and Georgian personnel will begin a dialogue on control of movement in Georgian air space.

Implementation of these coordination plans are said to require 23 joint American-Georgian maneuvers.[6] In addition, the European Command (EUCOM) has committed to military assistance programs in Azerbaijan, Georgia, Uzbekistan, and Kyrgyzstan.

Working with local air forces will present a difficult task. In general, these forces are underdeveloped and in poor condition. Kyrgyzstan, Tajikistan, Armenia, and Georgia do not yet have viable independent air forces.[7] Azerbaijan has only a modest and outdated air force. Kazakhstan has a large inventory of modern fighters and bombers as well as Mi-24 Hind attack helicopters, but faces resource shortages that have led to low maintenance, training, and support levels.[8] Uzbekistan has the best maintained and funded air force in the region, with a mix of outmoded MiG-21s and more sophisticated MiG-29 interceptor jets. It also has Su-27s for close air support and a transport inventory of outdated An-2s, An-26s, and Mi-8 helicopters.[9] Flying hours for all these air forces, however, are low or nonexistent,[10] budgets for maintenance and logistical support are low, and airfields are not well kept.

In an environment in which the USAF faces real budget constraints of its own, specific training programs and military-to-military contacts should be selected based upon lessons learned from previous military security assistance programs targeted at the European the-

---

[6]Sanobar Shermatova, "Caspian Faces Threat of Militarization," *Moskovskiye Novosti,* April 19–26, 1998.

[7]Kyrgyzstan inherited 2400 aircraft and helicopters but has since traded its air fleet to Uzbekistan in a debt swap and has lost aircraft to Russian repatriation. Tajikistan has announced plans to form an air force squadron and to acquire SU-25s from Belarus. Georgia, too, has a small number of SU-25 aircraft and several transport helicopters, and has supplemented these assets with a composite regiment of transport aircraft and helicopters. Armenia has not yet developed an independent air force. It has one attack helicopter squadron and six combat aircraft assigned to the army. Each of these countries also has remnants of the Soviet air defense system in the form of small stocks of SA-2, SA-3, and SA-5 surface-to-air missiles.

[8]Kazakhstan, for example, currently has one heavy bomber regiment, one division with three fighter-bomber regiments, and single independent reconnaissance, fighter, and helicopter regiments.

[9]Data for Central Asia and the south Caucasus are based on declarations of equipment holdings under the CFE Treaty and are taken from *The Military Balance 1997–1998,* International Institute for Strategic Studies, Oxford University Press, Oxford, 1998.

[10]The only state to report flying hours was Kazakhstan with 25.

ater. First priority should be accorded to the most viable regional military powers: Uzbekistan, Kazakhstan, and Azerbaijan. Secondary priority should be given to those second-tier countries that show improvements in their transitions to Western-style democratic systems and market economies (Georgia and Kyrgyzstan). These programs should not be allowed, however, to slide into security commitments.

For example, a constructive step the USAF can take is to improve training and education systems for officers and technical education programs for military occupational specialists. This goal can be partially attained through EUCOM programs like the George C. Marshall European Center and increased International Military Education and Training (IMET) programs aimed at enhancing professional military competence, expanding the recipients' knowledge of U.S. military principles, and furnishing the skills essential to stable civil-military relationships in periods of nation-building.[11] However, traditional IMET-funded training in Central Europe has been costly and limited in scope because of reliance on U.S. schooling. Instead, military training assistance teams (MATs) could be sent to these countries. This has proven to be an effective and low-cost approach and has correlated with improved access to foreign military bases, facilities, and air space.[12] The new NATO members, familiar with the challenges of converting Soviet forces to usable national forces and with a good working knowledge of the specific assets, would be valuable additions to such a team. MAT teams could provide guidance in defense planning for these countries. An example of the need for defense planning, if indeed the security challenges are largely internal and regional, might be a shift from fixed-wing aircraft to increased helicopter assets.

---

[11]IMET programs have been available to participating countries of Central Asia and the south Caucasus, but funding has remained nominal and the level of participation small, especially beyond English-language training programs in in-country language labs. See William O'Malley, "Defense Cooperation and Security Assistance: Lessons and Implications," paper prepared for the RAND Conference on Central Asia and the Caucasus, April 1998.

[12]Adapted from a recent report by David M. Glantz, *Advancing United States and European Security: United States Military Assistance to Poland, the Czech Republic, and Hungary,* Office of the Secretary of Defense, February 1998.

CRISIS MANAGEMENT AND PEACEKEEPING

A Caspian region torn by conflict and upheaval would have a profound impact on the Eurasian geopolitical landscape. As Graham Fuller has noted, there are numerous possibilities for violence, conflict, and instability in and around the borders of the region that could threaten the security and stability of the Caspian states, provoke outside military intervention, or spill over to destabilize neighboring countries (see Figure 7). Possibilities for tensions or conflict might involve

- Russia and the republics over ethnic, territorial, or resource questions, especially in Kazakhstan, or Russian attempts to restore order or empire if the region plunges into general chaos;

- China and Kazakhstan, Kyrgyzstan, Tajikistan, or Russia over potential ethnic separatism within the Turkic population in Xinjiang;

- Afghanistan and Tajikistan, Turkmenistan, and Uzbekistan if the breakup of Afghanistan leads to the redrawing of national boundaries between these countries along ethnic lines;

- Iran and Azerbaijan and Turkmenistan over ethnic issues, Iranian meddling in Azeri internal affairs, or an Azeri-supported secessionist movement in Iranian Azerbaijan;

- Turkey and Armenia should the latter gain the upper hand in its conflict with Azerbaijan;

- the Caspian states themselves over borders, resources, and ethno/nationalist differences; and

- internal conflicts arising from separatist movements (e.g., rebellion in Georgia).[13]

---

[13]Graham E. Fuller, "Russia and Central Asia: Federation or Fault Line?" in Michael Mandelbaum (ed.) (1994), p. 104.

RAND *MR1074-7*

Figure 7—Potential Flashpoints

In addition to these scenarios, conflict among and within the Central Asian states could provoke outside intervention. Among the most likely possibilities are border disputes and ethnic irredentism involving Uzbekistan and all its Central Asian neighbors, a resumption of hostilities between Azerbaijan and Armenia over Nagorno-Karabakh, and the implosion of Tajikistan and possible outside intervention by others (e.g., Iran, Afghanistan).

Because these conflicts would threaten the West's general interest in stability, or could create humanitarian crises, the United States and many of its allies would feel pressure to help prevent, resolve, or contain these conflicts, although in many situations Western influence would be limited. That said, conflict in Central Asia and the south Caucasus is a necessary but not sufficient condition for the employment of NATO military assets. For these conflicts to be of a sufficient challenge to Western interests to warrant consideration of a military response, several conditions would have to be met. The conflict would need to (1) threaten the independence and territorial integrity of a state deemed important to NATO's own security and well-being; (2) raise a serious possibility that the victorious side would be in a position to assert hegemony over all or most of the region and thus gain control over energy resources; (3) jeopardize access not only to the energy resources of the Caspian region but also to the Persian Gulf, since loss of the former without a serious disruption of the latter would probably be manageable through market adjustments; or (4) threaten the security and stability of a NATO member or countries of importance to NATO.

When these criteria are applied, many potential threats and conflicts in the region have little or no military/security implications for NATO, even though they may have unfortunate consequences for the states involved or create large-scale turmoil. Examples might be (1) internal conflicts among clans, tribes, ethnic groups, or regions over control of power, land, water, and energy resources; (2) interstate conflicts arising from ethnic or territorial disputes, such as attempts by the Uzbeks to adjust their national borders with Tajikistan or Kyrgyzstan; (3) the spillover of conflict between Tajikistan and Afghanistan; (4) nationalist/religious unrest in China's XUAR that could prompt Chinese attempts to intervene militarily in Tajikistan or Kyrgyzstan; and (5) civil wars or ethnic conflicts that pose no risk of escalating beyond the borders of the state involved.

At the same time, these criteria for NATO involvement in dealing with regional threats suggest that over the next 10–15 years several possible scenarios for interstate conflict and external intervention could impinge on NATO security interests. In addition to devising political and diplomatic strategies to deal with these challenges, it may also be appropriate for NATO to consider a more active role in conflict prevention and perhaps engage in low-key military planning for crisis management and peacekeeping. An illustrative, but by no means exhaustive, menu of scenarios is sketched out below:

- **South Caucasus.** Unlike Central Asia, the south Caucasus borders NATO territory. Therefore, there is a risk that regional conflict there could spill over into Turkey or precipitate Turkish military involvement. For example, a resumption of full-scale hostilities between Armenia and Azerbaijan, or conflict between Iran and Azerbaijan that threatened Azerbaijan's territorial integrity, could invite Turkish intervention. Another scenario could involve Turkish military assistance to Georgia in the event that Turkish-Georgian ties and pipelines carrying Caspian oil across Georgia to Turkish ports on the Mediterranean were being disrupted by internal conflict in Georgia. A Turkish-Iranian conflict in the south Caucasus, in particular, could prove to be highly destabilizing, and the eruption of a messy conflict in a region bordering NATO could push the United States and its NATO allies toward some form of military involvement. Moreover, by 2010–2015 Romania and possibly Bulgaria and Ukraine may be members of NATO, which would focus Western interests even more strongly on the south Caucasus, especially if these countries serve as an access route for Caspian oil. In fact, the emerging association of Georgia, Ukraine, Uzbekistan, Azerbaijan, and Moldova is likely to lead to deeper Turkish involvement in the region and possibly participation in this or some other regional configuration.

- **Russia-Kazakhstan.** Because Kazakhstan is one of the largest energy producers in the region and a bulwark against a revival of Russian neo-imperialism, its independence and territorial integrity are important to NATO. The presence of a large and increasingly disenchanted Russian minority in Kazakhstan's border areas adjacent to Russia is potentially volatile. President Nazarbayev has so far managed to keep a lid on extreme manifestations of both Russian and Kazakh nationalism. However, his eventual disappearance, the absence of a viable succession mechanism, and the rise of Kazakh nationalism portend a substantial risk of raised tensions with ethnic Russians, which could trigger Russian military intervention, the possible secession of Kazakhstan's northern provinces, or even Russian occupation of the country.

- **Iranian Expansionism.** It is difficult to envision a conflict in the Caspian region that could spill over to threaten the unimpeded flow of Persian Gulf oil or the security of a Gulf state that mattered to NATO (e.g., Saudi Arabia or Kuwait). Nonetheless, in the 2010–2015 time frame, the possibility of a militarily strong and expansionist Iran cannot be ruled out. If this development were to coincide with simultaneous regime crises in Saudi Arabia and Azerbaijan, a serious threat to vital Western interests could emerge. For example, a full-scale civil war in Azerbaijan with one faction supported by Tehran, combined with a prolonged and violent succession crisis in Saudi Arabia marked by large-scale Islamic unrest and plummeting Saudi oil production, could provoke Iranian military intervention in both countries in a bid to achieve Iran's long-standing goal of regional domination. If Iranian-sponsored regimes seized power in Riyadh and Baku, Iran would be in a position to control a significant portion of the world's energy resources.

- **Reassertion of Russian Hegemony.** Although it is unlikely that in the near to medium term Russia will regain the capabilities to restore its empire in the region, in the 2010–2015 time frame, it is possible to envision the interaction of two variables that might put extreme pressure on Moscow to use force on a large scale. First, widespread chaos that raised the specter of encircling Russia with hostile regimes, especially in the south Caucasus; and second, a dramatic reversal of Russia's declining economic and military fortunes. Under these circumstances, there would be a significant risk that a highly nationalistic Russian government with a modernized military would engage in neo-imperialist intervention. While such a scenario appears unlikely, it is not inconceivable if things really go wrong.

In light of the multiple possibilities for messy ethnic and regional conflicts, the international community can probably expect increased pressure for the deployment of peacekeeping forces. Whether NATO has a role to play in these contingencies, either as an independent actor or as part of a broader coalition within the framework of the UN, OSCE, or CIS, raises sensitive issues with Russia and within NATO.

As previously noted, Russia is extremely sensitive to any perceived "meddling" in what Moscow regards as a Russian sphere of influence in the southern CIS tier. Accordingly, any NATO effort to play an independent role in peacekeeping and "security management" is bound to elicit an extremely negative Russian reaction that could halt or reverse the long-term trend of Russian disengagement. Apart from Russian opposition, there would be other constraints on an independent NATO peacekeeping role. First, because many NATO countries regard the south Caucasus and Central Asia as areas of peripheral concern, it would be difficult to gain NATO consensus on a peacekeeping operation, especially if such an operation carried a substantial risk of high costs and casualties and long duration. Second, for these and related reasons, there would be considerable domestic opposition in the United States and elsewhere to a NATO peacekeeping role in the region.

Even though an independent NATO peacekeeping role in the Caspian region is highly unlikely under current and foreseeable circumstances, the possibility cannot be ruled out that NATO might be called upon to contribute to peacekeeping operations. In this connection, it is important to remember that in 1992 the Alliance offered to support OSCE peacekeeping missions, including making NATO assets available on a case-by-case basis. In the future, therefore, NATO could face OSCE requests to provide military capabilities in support of OSCE peacekeeping. Other illustrative requirements in regional contingencies include airlift operations in support of disaster relief or humanitarian intervention, sanctions enforcement, monitoring of demilitarized zones, military activities along borders, cease-fires, and disarmament agreements, and the deployment of a Macedonia-type peacekeeping force, for example, along the borders between Armenia and Azerbaijan or Azerbaijan and Iran. NATO operations in these scenarios will face formidable challenges, however. For instance, the military stocks and infrastructure of local states are not well suited to peacekeeping missions. Consequently, over the next 10–15 years, there are only fair to poor prospects for successful interoperability with NATO and other Western forces, and limited airstrips that Western air forces might use for peacekeeping operations.

The prospects for NATO participation in an OSCE-led peacekeeping operation in the southern CIS states—or, for that matter, any independent OSCE peacekeeping operation in the region—are dim for the foreseeable future. It is true that Moscow has recently taken a more favorable view toward an OSCE role in mediating some of the region's more intractable conflicts. There is also evidence that Moscow is growing weary of the financial and manpower costs of CIS peacekeeping operations, particularly in Abkhazia. Nonetheless, the Russians remain leery of any non-Russian peacekeeping operations in the CIS and have yet to agree, for example, on any OSCE supervision of a peacekeeping operation in the CIS.[14] More important, the risk of NATO involvement in a quagmire is not justified by this region's marginal importance.

As a matter of both principle and policy, Russia will almost certainly oppose any joint peacekeeping operations with NATO in its "near abroad" for at least the next several years, even if Russia were in command and NATO the junior partner. In the future, if CIS peacekeeping puts more of a strain on Russia, and depending on the overall state of the NATO-Russian relationship, Moscow might explore other arrangements for sharing the responsibilities and burdens of security management, including the possibility of Russian-NATO joint peacekeeping under the umbrella of the UN, OSCE, NATO, or the CIS. Such a fundamental shift in Russian attitudes toward NATO's military involvement in the region is unlikely to occur, however, for at least the next 5–10 years, if it takes place at all. In the meantime, Russia is likely to view the OSCE as a more preferable alternative to NATO for peacekeeping operations in the CIS. Accordingly, until Russia softens its view toward a NATO role in Central Asian peacekeeping operations, any NATO planning for such efforts should be undertaken only as part of a broader dialogue with Russia and the OSCE on security issues and peacekeeping cooperation in the south Caucasus and Central Asia. Once the damage inflicted by Kosovo on the NATO-Russian relationship is repaired, the NATO-Russian Joint Permanent Council—or perhaps the EAPC—may be a suitable venue for such a dialogue.

In sum, the vast majority of potential intra- and interstate conflicts and instabilities either pose no threat to major Western interests or are not readily amenable to military solutions or Western influence. Nevertheless, a handful of conflicts are imaginable that might merit attention by U.S. and NATO planners, because they could threaten the security and stability of Turkey or the independence of key Caspian states. The possibility of a Turkish-Iranian confrontation in the south Caucasus would pose the most serious dilemma for NATO.

---

[14]For a thorough discussion of Russian peacekeeping policy in the CIS that highlights Moscow's sensitivity to outside involvement, see N. A. Kellett, *Russian Peacekeeping Part II: The Strategic Context,* Canadian Department of National Defense, Research Note 96/08, Ottawa, Canada, December 1996.

On the one hand, Turkey is a member of NATO, and a failure by the Alliance to come to Turkey's defense in the event it were attacked by Iran could lead to Turkey's withdrawal from NATO and might damage the cohesion of the Atlantic Alliance. On the other hand, the south Caucasus remains peripheral to the core security interests of most members of the Alliance and there will be a strong impulse to avoid getting dragged into a confrontation with Iran, particularly in light of Iran's geopolitical importance. Further, the circumstances surrounding a Turkish-Iranian conflict in the south Caucasus are likely to be ambiguous, making it difficult to identify aggressor and victim or the merits of each side's conflicting claims. Under these circumstances, NATO military support for Turkey should not be taken for granted. It is precisely for this reason that the West and NATO should give priority to resolving the underlying problems that, if left to fester, might cause the Turkish-Iranian competition for influence in the Caucasus to spin out of control.

MAJOR MILITARY OPERATIONS

The possibility that the Caspian states could face external threats to their security or internal destabilization, or that ethnic and regional conflicts could jeopardize access to the region's energy resources, raises the question of what role, if any, NATO's force projection capabilities might play in responding to these threats. For a variety of reasons, it is difficult to discern any significant implications of the changing strategic environment in the Caspian region for NATO's security commitments, military plans, or force posture, at least for the next decade.

- Because the West will not become dependent on Caspian oil for the foreseeable future, a disruption of Caspian oil supplies would not warrant NATO military intervention to restore access.

- The most serious challenges to stability and Western security interests—political, social, economic, ethnic, religious grievances, organized crime, corruption, narcotics, and trafficking—do not lend themselves to the application of NATO's military force.

- With the important exception of a regional conflict escalating to attacks on Turkish territory, which appears unlikely, most of the region's conflicts are likely to remain localized, and those with the potential to spread (e.g., civil war in Tajikistan) would have no great strategic significance for NATO.

- It is extremely unlikely that NATO will extend security guarantees to any of the states in Central Asia or the south Caucasus or offer prospective membership in the Alliance. Although there is general Western support for the independence of these states, it is hard to make the case that the preservation of their independence is critical to Western security. Indeed, it would be exceptionally difficult, perhaps even impossible, to garner a consensus within NATO that the independence of any of these states is a "vital" interest.

- Given the limited nature of Western interests, the fear of antagonizing Russia, the prospects of high costs and casualties, and the escalatory risks of introducing NATO forces, there would be strong opposition within the Alliance to military intervention in the Caspian.

- There is no consensus within NATO on the Alliance's role in the region, and it is unrealistic to expect NATO to assume major security responsibilities there. For now, as one prominent expert on the region has observed, "NATO is satisfied with providing limited training assistance and symbolic demonstrations of Western capacity."[15]

In conclusion, the emerging security environment in Central Asia and the south Caucasus has minimal implications for NATO. Notwithstanding much of the hyperbole over the discovery of energy resources in the region and the rivalry for geopolitical influence, NATO and the West do not have vital interests at stake in the Caspian region. Moreover, the growing Western interests in the region—preventing a single power from gaining regional hegemony, preserving access to energy, preventing the spread of WMD and the spillover of conflict to important countries—are not endangered in the current threat environment. Further, these interests are best protected in the long run by a Western strategy that relies primarily on political, economic, and energy measures to eradicate the sources of conflict and

---

[15]Olcott (Summer 1998), p. 111.

instability that could trigger large-scale civil strife, military confrontations, and outside intervention.

Because there is no significant role for NATO to play in responding to the threats and opportunities in the emerging Caspian security environment over the next decade, the Alliance does not need to consider major changes in force planning or force structure in response to developments in the region. Furthermore, NATO faces serious limitations on its ability to project influence and solve the area's most difficult challenges. The key objectives of Western policy should be to promote democratic reform, market economies, and nation-building. NATO does not command the resources to advance these objectives and thus has little value-added to offer. Other organizations, such as the EU, OSCE, UN, and international financial institutions, as well as bilateral trade, aid, and investment, can make a greater contribution to achieving these objectives. Although modest NATO peacetime military activities are beneficial, they have thus far had only a marginal impact on improving the security and stability of the Central Asian and south Caucasus states, and by no means have a unique role to play in expanding contacts with the West or diversifying the relationships and options of these countries. Moreover, a high NATO profile would spark a hostile Russian reaction that would complicate efforts to forge a constructive partnership with Russia.

Indeed, the West will need to remain sensitive to Russia's legitimate security interests and NATO's goal of developing a cooperative partnership with Russia. Managing the Russian dimension of a Caspian security strategy poses a dilemma for NATO: on the one hand, the Alliance has a strong interest in preventing the forced reintegration of the former Soviet south into the CIS and in ensuring that these countries remain open to the outside world; on the other hand, Russia is extremely sensitive to any perceived meddling in what Moscow regards as a Russian sphere of influence, and Russia can still cause problems for many of the states in the region. Russian touchiness over NATO activities in the Caspian has only been inflamed by its perceived humiliation in Kosovo at the hands of NATO.

Consequently, there is great risk that an aggressive NATO effort to expand its engagement—particularly high-profile military activities with Turkey—would be perceived by Moscow as an anti-Russian containment strategy, provoking a backlash that could endanger Western objectives and halt or reverse the long-term trend of Russian disengagement. The challenge for NATO is to give Russia a growing stake in regional stability and nudge it in the direction of moderation, without appearing threatening and bringing about the very reaction the West is trying to avoid. Ultimately, what the West wants for the region—political stability, economic development, and prosperity—is as much in Russia's interest as in the West's.

Most members of the Alliance will be reluctant to take on additional security and military responsibilities in the Caspian Zone or act as a regional policeman. Simply put, NATO's interests there and the threats to those interests are not commensurate with the Alliance aspiring to play a major security role in the Caspian. Inasmuch as the Alliance lacks the collective interest, will, capabilities, and resources to assume responsibility for Caspian security, a U.S.-led coalition of willing countries rather than NATO should assume primary responsibility for securing Western objectives in the Caspian basin. Given the meager benefits and potentially high costs of extending NATO's security responsibilities in the region, the Alliance's more pressing priorities, and finite resources and commitments, deepening NATO's engagement in the Caspian region should not command a high priority in terms of resources, planning, or attention. Instead, NATO should concentrate on the other tasks and challenges on its security agenda for the 21st century.

BIBLIOGRAPHY

Ahrari, M. E., *The New Great Game in Muslim Central Asia*, McNair Paper 47, National Defense University Press, Washington, DC, January 1996.

Anjaparidze, Zaal, "Negotiability Versus Negotiations: Georgia and the Abhaz Question," *Jamestown Prism*, Vol. 4, No. 6, Part 4, March 20, 1998.

Arvanitopoulos, Constantine, "The Geopolitics of Oil in Central Asia," *Thesis*, Vol. 1, Issue No. 4, Winter 1997–1998, pp. 18–27.

"Azerbaijan Accuses China of Selling Secrets to Armenia," *Radio Free Europe/Radio Liberty Newsline*, Vol. 3, No. 97, Part I, May 19, 1999.

Banuazizi, Ali, and Myron Weiner (eds.), *The New Geopolitics of Central Asia and Its Borderlands*, I. B. Tauris, London and New York, 1994.

Becker, Abraham S., "Russia and the Caucasus-Central Asia States: Why is Moscow Floundering?" paper prepared for the RAND Conference on Security Dynamics in Central Asia and the Caucasus, March 1998.

Blandy, C. W., *Oil is Not the Only Stake*, Conflict Studies Research Center, Report S28, Camberley, Surrey, February 1997.

Blank, Stephen J., *Energy, Economics, and Security in Central Asia: Russia and Its Rivals*, Strategic Studies Institute, U.S. Army War College, Carlisle Barracks, PA, 1995.

_____, "Russia's Back in Central Asia," *Middle East Quarterly*, June 1995, pp. 55–61.

_____, "Russia's Real Drive to the South," *Orbis*, Summer 1995, JAI Press for the Foreign Policy Research Institute, Greenwich, CT, pp. 369–386.

_____, *Energy and Security in South Caucasus*, Strategic Studies Institute, U.S. Army War College, Carlisle Barracks, PA, September 1994.

Bolukbasi, Suha, "Ankara's Baku-Centered Transcaucasian Policy: Has It Failed?" *Middle East Journal*, Vol. 51, No. 1, Winter 1997, pp. 80–94.

Bremmer, Ian, and Ray Taras (eds.), *Nations and Politics in the Soviet Successor States*, Cambridge University Press, New York, 1992.

Brown, Bess A., "Security Concerns of the Central Asian States," in Jed C. Snyder (ed.), *After Empire: The Emerging Geopolitics of Central Asia*, NDU Press, Washington, DC, 1995.

Brzezinski, Zbigniew, "The Eurasian Balkans," in *The Grand Chessboard*, Basic Books, New York, 1997.

_____, "A Geostrategy for Eurasia," *Foreign Affairs*, September/ October 1997, pp. 51–64.

Bunce, Valerie, "Regional Differences in Democratization: The East Versus the South," *Post-Soviet Affairs*, Vol. 14, No. 3, July– September 1998, pp. 187–212.

Central Intelligence Agency, *Atlas of the Middle East*, U.S. Government Printing Office, Washington, DC, January 1983.

_____, *Handbook of International Economic Statistics*, U.S. Government Printing Office, Washington, DC, September 1992.

Chang, Felix, "China's Central Asian Power and Problems," *Orbis*, Vol. 41, No. 3, Summer 1997, pp. 401–425.

Christoffersen, Gaye, "China's Intentions for Russian and Central Asian Oil and Gas," *The National Bureau of Asian Research*, Vol. 9, No. 2, March 1998.

Clark, Susan, "The Central Asian States: Defining Security Priorities and Developing Military Forces," in Michael Mandelbaum (ed.), *Central Asia and the World*, Council on Foreign Relations, New York, 1994.

Clawson, Patrick, "The Former Soviet South and the Muslim World," in Jed C. Snyder (ed.), *After Empire: The Emerging Geopolitics of Central Asia*, NDU Press, Washington, DC, 1995.

_____, "Energy Security in a Time of Plenty," Strategic Forum Paper No. 130, NDU Press, Washington, D.C, October 1997.

_____, "Iran and Caspian Basin Oil and Gas," *Perceptions*, December 1997–February 1998, pp. 17–27.

Cohen, Ariel, *The New 'Great Game': Oil Politics in the Caucasus and Central Asia*, The Heritage Foundation Backgrounder No. 1065, Washington, DC, January 25, 1996.

_____, "The New 'Great Game': Pipeline Politics in Eurasia," *Eurasian Studies*, Vol. 3, No. 1, Spring 1996, pp. 2–15.

_____, *U.S. Policy in the Caucasus and Central Asia: Building a New "Silk Road" to Economic Prosperity*, The Heritage Foundation Backgrounder No. 1132, Washington, DC, July 24, 1997.

Cornell, Svante E., "Turkey and the Conflict in Nagorno-Karabakh: A Delicate Balance," *Middle Eastern Studies*, Vol. 34, No. 1, January 1998, pp. 51–72.

Croissant, Cynthia M., and Michael P. Croissant, "The Caspian Sea Status Dispute: Context and Legal Implications," *Eurasian Studies*, Vol. 3, No. 4, Winter 1996/97, pp. 23–40.

Croissant, Michael P., "Oil and Russian Imperialism in the Transcaucasus," *Eurasian Studies*, Vol. 3, No. 1, Spring 1996, pp. 16–26.

Crow, Suzanne, "Russia Promotes the CIS as an International Organization," *RFE/RL Research Report*, Vol. 3, No. 11, March 1994, pp. 33–38.

Cullen, Robert, "Central Asia and the West," in *Central Asia and the World*, Michael Mandelbaum (ed.), Council on Foreign Relations, New York, 1994.

Curtis, Glenn (ed.), *Kazakhstan, Kyrgyzstan, Tajikistan, Turkmenistan, and Uzbekistan: Country Studies*, Federal Research Division of the Library of Congress, Washington, DC, March 1996.

Danielyan, Emil, "Ten Years Since the Start of Karabakh Movement," *Radio Free Europe/Radio Liberty Daily Report*, February 20, 1998.

_____, "Velvet Coup Promises Sweeping Changes in Armenia," *Radio Free Europe/Radio Liberty Daily Report*, February 23, 1998.

Dannreuther, Roland, "Russia, Central Asia, and the Persian Gulf," *Survival*, Vol. 35, No. 4, Winter 1993, pp. 92–112.

_____, *Creating New States in Central Asia*, Adelphi Paper 288, Oxford University Press for IISS, Oxford, 1994.

Ebel, Robert E., *Energy Choices in the Near Abroad: The Haves and the Have-Nots Face the Future*, The Center for Strategic and International Studies, Washington, DC, April 1997.

_____, "Geopolitics and Pipelines," *Analysis of Current Events*, Vol. 9, No. 2, February 1997, pp. 1–3.

Ellison, Herbert J., and Bruce A. Acker, "Azerbaijan: U.S. Policy Options," National Bureau of Asian Research Briefing, June 1997, pp. 1–9.

Emerson, Sarah A., "The Relevance of Caspian Oil for the World," paper prepared for the Fourth Annual Energy Conference on Caspian Resources, The Emirates Center for Strategic Studies and Research, October 1998.

Finberg, Jared, "GUAM's Potential Outside of the CIS," *Weekly Defense Monitor*, Center for Defense Information, May 24–31, 1997.

Forsythe, Rosemarie, *The Politics of Oil in the Caucasus and Central Asia*, Adelphi Paper 300, Oxford University Press for IISS, Oxford, 1996.

Fraij, Hanna Yousif, "State Interests vs. The Umma: Iranian Policy in Central Asia," *Middle East Journal*, Vol. 50, No. 1, Winter 1996, pp. 71–83.

Freedman, Robert O., "Russia and Iran: A Tactical Alliance," *SAIS Review*, Vol. 17, No. 2, Summer–Fall 1997, pp. 93–109.

Fuller, Elizabeth, "The Tussle for Influence in Central Asia and the South Caucasus," *Transition*, June 14, 1996, pp. 11–15.

_____, "Why Kill Shevardnadze?" *Radio Free Europe/Radio Liberty Daily Report*, February 17, 1998.

Fuller, Graham E., *Central Asia: The New Geopolitics*, RAND, R-4219-USDP, 1992.

_____, *Turkey Faces East: New Orientations Toward the Middle East and the Old Soviet Union*, RAND, R-4232-AF/A, 1992.

_____, "Central Asia: The Quest for Identity," *Current History*, Vol. 93, No. 582, April 1994, pp. 145–149.

_____, "The New Geopolitical Order," in Ali Banuazizi and Myron Weiner (eds.), *The New Geopolitics of Central Asia and Its Borderlands*, Indiana University Press, Bloomington, 1994.

_____, "Russia and Central Asia: Federation or Fault Line?" in Michael Mandelbaum (ed.), *Central Asia and the World*, Council on Foreign Relations, New York, 1994.

Garnett, Sherman, "Russia and the Former Soviet South," *Central Asia Monitor*, No. 6, 1998.

George, Bruce, "NATO, OSCE, and Regional Security Issues in Central Asia and the Caucasus," *Perceptions*, December 1997–February 1998, pp. 135–142.

Glantz, David M., *Advancing United States and European Security. United States Military Assistance to Poland, the Czech Republic, and Hungary*, Office of the Secretary of Defense, February 1998.

Goble, Paul, "Pipeline and Pipedreams: The Geo-Politics of the Transcaucasus," *Caspian Crossroads*, Vols. 1–2, Winter 1995–Spring 1997, pp. 3–6.

_____, "From Myths to Maps: American Interests in the Countries of Central Asia and the Caucasus," *Caspian Crossroads*, Vol. 3, No. 1, Summer 1997.

_____, "Why Ter-Petrossyan Fell," *Interfax Electronic Daily Report*, February 6, 1998.

_____, "Caspian: Analysis from Washington—Pipelines Under Troubled Waters," *Radio Free Europe/Radio Liberty Daily Report*, July 10, 1998.

_____, "New Moves on the Caucasus Chessboard," *Radio Free Europe/Radio Liberty Daily Report*, April 16, 1999.

Goltz, Thomas, "Catch-907 in the Caucasus," *The National Interest*, No. 48, Summer 1997, pp. 37–45.

Goodby, James E., "Loose Nukes: Security Issues on the U.S.-Russian Agenda," an Arthur and Frank Payne Lecture, Institute for International Studies, Stanford University, April 10, 1997.

Gorst, Isabel, and Nina Poussenkova, "Petroleum Ambassadors of Russia: State Versus Corporate Policy in the Caspian Region," paper prepared for the James A. Baker III Institute for Public Policy, Rice University, 1998.

Hamilton, Rep. Lee (D-Ind), statement cited in *Journal of Commerce*, July 14, 1998.

Harris, Lillian Craig, "Xinjiang, Central Asia, and the Implications for China's Policy in the Islamic World," *The China Quarterly*, No. 133, March 1993, pp. 130–151.

Hearings on International Organized Crime and Its Impact on the United States, Senate Hearing 103-899, Senate Permanent Subcommittee on Investigations, 103d Congress, 2d Session, 1994.

Helmer, John, "Kazakhstan/Russia: Caspian Oil Disputes Linger," *Radio Free Europe/Radio Liberty Daily Report*, May 13, 1998.

Herzig, Edmund, *Iran and the Former Soviet South*, Royal Institute of International Affairs, London, 1995.

Heslin, Sheila N., "Key Constraints to Caspian Pipeline Development: Status, Significance, and Outlook," paper prepared for the James A. Baker III Institute for Public Policy, Rice University, 1998.

Hunter, Shireen T., "The Muslim Republics of the Former Soviet Union: Policy Challenges for the United States," *The Washington Quarterly*, Summer 1992, pp. 57–71.

_____, *Central Asia Since Independence*, The Washington Papers/168, Praeger Press, Westport, CT, with the Center for Strategic and International Studies, Washington, DC, 1996.

International Institute for Strategic Studies, "Caspian Oil: Not the Great Game Revisited," *Strategic Survey 1997/98*, London, 1998, pp. 22–29.

_____, *The Military Balance 1997–1998*, Oxford University Press, Oxford, 1998.

Jaffe, Amy Myers, "Unlocking the Assets: Energy and the Future of Central Asia and the Caucasus," paper prepared for the James A. Baker III Institute for Public Policy, Rice University, 1998.

Jaffe, Amy Myers, and Robert A. Manning, "The Myth of the Caspian 'Great Game': The Real Geopolitics of Oil," *Survival*, Vol. 40, No. 4, Winter 1998–1999, pp. 112–129.

Joseph, Ira B., "Caspian Gas Exports: Stranded Reserves in a Unique Predicament," Paper prepared for the James A. Baker III Institute, Rice University, 1998.

Jukes, Geoffrey, "Central Asia: The Soviet Heritage and Future Relations with Russia," *Russian and Euro-Asian Bulletin*, No. 7, July 1997.

Kangas, Roger, "With an Eye on Russia, Central Asian Militaries Practice Cooperation," *Transition*, Vol. 2, No. 16, August 9, 1996.

Kellett, N. A., *Russian Peacekeeping Part II: The Strategic Context*, Canadian Department of National Defense, Research Note 96/08, Ottawa, Canada, December 1996.

Kemp, Geoffrey, and Robert E. Harkavy, *The Strategic Geography of the Changing Middle East*, Carnegie Endowment for International Peace, Washington, DC, May 1997.

Khalilzad, Zalmay, "Why the West Needs Turkey," *The Wall Street Journal*, December 22, 1997.

Khripunov, Igor, and Mary M. Matthews, "Russia's Oil and Gas Interest Group and Its Foreign Policy Agenda," *Problems of Post-Communism*, May/June 1996, pp. 38–48.

Kortunov, Andrei, "Russia and Central Asia: Evolution of Mutual Perceptions, Policies, Interdependence," paper prepared for the James A. Baker III Institute for Public Policy, Rice University, 1998.

Kosto, Pal, "Anticipating Demographic Superiority: Kazakh Thinking on National Integration and Nation Building," *Europe-Asia Studies*, Vol. 50, No. 1, pp. 51–69.

Kovalev, Feliks, "Caspian Oil: Russian Interests," *International Affairs* (Moscow), Vol. 43, No. 3, Spring 1997, pp. 48–54.

Laitin, David D., "Language and Nationalism in the Post-Soviet Republics," *Post-Soviet Affairs*, Vol. 12, No. 1, January–March 1996, pp. 4–25.

Lelyveld, Michael, "Russia: Moscow's New Caspian Policy," *Radio Free Europe/Radio Liberty Daily Report*, April 7, 1998.

Larrabee, F. Stephen, "U.S. and European Policy Toward Turkey and the Caspian Basin," in Robert D. Blackwill and Michael Stürmer (eds.), *Allies Divided: Transatlantic Policies for the Greater Middle East*, The MIT Press, Cambridge, MA, 1997.

Lenczowski, George, "The Caspian Oil and Gas Basin: A New Source of Wealth," *Middle East Policy*, Vol. 5, No. 1, January 1997, pp. 111–119.

Leppingwell, John W.R., "The Russian Military and Security Policy in the Near Abroad," *Survival*, Vol. 36, No. 3, Autumn 1994, pp. 70–92.

Lesser, Ian, "Turkey: In Search of a Post–Cold War Role," *Private View*, Vol. 1/2, No. 4/5, Autumn 1997, pp. 90–96.

Lubin, Nancy, "New Security Threats in the Southern Tier," in Rajan Menon, Yuri Fyodorov, and Ghia Nodia (eds.), *Russia, the Caucasus, and Central Asia: The 21st Century Security Environment*, M. E. Sharpe, Armonk, NY, 1999.

Mandelbaum, Michael (ed.), *Central Asia and the World*, Council on Foreign Relations, New York, 1994.

Mark, David E., "Eurasia Letter: Russia and the New Transcaucasus," *Foreign Policy*, Carnegie Endowment for International Peace, Washington, DC, No. 105, Winter 1996–1997, pp. 141–159.

McFaul, Michael, "A Precarious Peace: Domestic Politics in the Making of Russian Foreign Policy," *International Security*, Vol. 22, No. 3, Winter 1997/1998, pp. 3–35.

Masanov, Nurbulat E., "The Clan Factor in Contemporary Political Life in Kazakhstan," translated by Mark Eckert, *Johnson's Russia List* (JRL), February 20, 1998.

Menon, Rajan, "In the Shadow of the Bear: Security in Post-Soviet Central Asia," *International Security*, Vol. 20, No. 1 Summer 1995, pp. 149–181.

_____, "Central Asia's Foreign Policy and Security Challenges: Implications for the United States," *National Bureau of Asian Research Analysis*, Vol. 6, No. 4, December 1995.

_____, "Treacherous Terrain: The Political and Security Dimensions of Energy Development in the Caspian Sea Zone," *The National Bureau of Asian Research Analysis*, Vol. 9, No. 1, February 1998.

_____, "After Empire: Russia and the Southern Near Abroad," in Michael Mandelbaum (ed.), *The New Russian Foreign Policy*, Council on Foreign Relations, New York, 1998.

Menon, Rajan, and Henri J. Barkey, "The Transformation of Central Asia: Implications for Regional and International Security," *Survival*, Vol. 34, No. 4, Winter 1992–93, pp. 68–89.

Menon, Rajan, Yuri Fyodorov, and Ghia Nodia (eds.), *Russia, the Caucasus, and Central Asia: The 21st Century Security Environment*, M. E. Sharpe, Armonk, NY, 1999.

Mesbahi, Mohiaddin, "Russian Foreign Policy and Security in Central Asia and the Caucasus," *Central Asian Survey*, Vol. 12, No. 2, 1993, pp. 181–215.

Minton-Beddoes, Zanny, "A Caspian Gamble," *The Economist*, February 7, 1998, p. 6 of insert.

Munro, Ross, "Central Asia and China," in Michael Mandelbaum (ed.), *Central Asia and the World*, Council on Foreign Relations, New York, 1994.

_____, "The Asian Interior, China's Waxing Spheres of Influence," *Orbis*, Vol. 35, No. 4, Fall 1994, pp. 585–605.

Olcott, Martha Brill, "Central Asia's Post-Empire Politics," *Orbis*, Spring 1992, pp. 253–268.

_____, "Central Asia's Catapult to Independence," *Foreign Affairs*, Summer 1992, pp. 108–130.

_____, "Ceremony and Substance: The Illusion of Unity in Central Asia," in Michael Mandelbaum (ed.), *Central Asia and the World*, Council on Foreign Relations Press, New York, 1994.

_____, *Central Asia's New States: Independence, Foreign Policy, and Regional Security*, United States Institute of Peace, Washington, DC, 1996.

_____, "The Central Asian States: An Overview of Five Years of Independence," testimony before Senate Foreign Relations Committee, Federal News Service, July 22, 1997.

_____, "The Caspian's False Promise," *Foreign Policy*, Carnegie Endowment for International Peace, Washington, DC, Summer 1998, pp. 95–112.

_____, "Central Asia: Confronting Independence," paper prepared for the James A. Baker III Institute for Public Policy, Rice University, Houston, TX, 1998.

O'Malley, William D., "Defense Cooperation and Security Assistance: Lessons and Implications," paper prepared for the RAND Conference on Central Asia and the Caucasus, April 1998.

O'Malley, William D., and Roman Solchanyk, *Central Asian Combined Peacekeeping Battalion: Preliminary Assessment and Recommendations*, RAND, DRU-1564-OSD, March 1997.

Parrish, Scott, "Chaos in Foreign Policy Decision-Making," *Transition*, May 17, 1996, pp. 30–31.

Parrott, Stuart, "Central Asia: Russia Reduces Its Role," *Radio Free Liberty/Radio Liberty Daily Report*, January 26, 1998.

Partridge, Ben, "Caucasus/Central Asia: Region Relies Too Much on Oil and Gas," *Radio Free Europe/Radio Liberty Daily Report*, April 14, 1998.

"Plan to Station More Russian Arms in Armenia Alarms Azerbaijan," *Jamestown Monitor* (electronic version), July 20, 1998.

Potter, William C., *Nuclear Profiles of the Soviet Successor States*, Monterey Institute of International Studies, Monterey, CA, May 1993.

Riva, Joseph P., Jr., "Petroleum in the Muslim Republics of the Commonwealth of Independent States: More Oil for OPEC?" Congressional Research Service Report, Washington, DC, September 1, 1992.

Roberts, John, *Caspian Pipelines*, Royal Institute of International Affairs, London, 1996.

Robins, Philip, "Between Sentiment and Self-Interest: Turkey's Policy Toward Azerbaijan and the Central Asian States," *Middle East Journal*, Vol. 47, No. 4, Autumn 1995, pp. 593–610.

Rozova, Marianna, "Caspian Boom: 21st Century Bubble?" *Moskovkiy Komsomolets*, March 19, 1998, p. 2.

Rumer, Boris Z., "The Gathering Storm in Central Asia," *Orbis*, Winter 1993, JAI Press for the Foreign Policy Research Institute, Greenwich, CT, pp. 89–105.

_____, "The Potential for Political Instability and Regional Conflicts," in Ali Banuazizi and Myron Weiner (eds.), *The New Geopolitics of Central Asia and Its Borderlands*, Indiana University Press, Bloomington, 1994.

_____ (ed.), *Central Asia in Transition*, M. E. Sharpe, Armonk, NY, 1996.

Rumer, Eugene B., *The Building Blocks of Russia's Future Military Doctrine*, RAND, MR-359-A, 1994.

Ruseckas, Laurent, "Caspian Oil: Getting Beyond the Great Game," *Analysis of Current Events*, Vol. 9, No. 2, February 1997, pp. 4–5.

_____, "Energy and Politics in Central Asia and the Caucasus, *National Bureau of Asian Research Analysis*, Vol. 1, No. 2, July 1998.

Sagan, Scott D., "Why Do States Build Nuclear Weapons?" *International Security*, Vol. 21, No. 3, Winter 1996/97, pp. 54–86.

Sajjadpour, S. K., "Iran, the Caucasus, and Central Asia," in Ali Banuazizi and Myron Weiner (eds.), *The New Geopolitics of Central Asia and Its Borderlands*, I. B. Tauris, London and New York, 1994.

Salameh, Mamdouh G., "China, Oil, and the Risk of Regional Conflict," *Survival*, Vol. 37, No. 4, Winter 1995–96, pp. 133–146.

Sharipzhan, Merhat, "Central Asia: New Developments in Russian Caspian Policy," *Radio Free Europe/Radio Liberty Daily Report*, April 17, 1998.

Shashenkov, Maxim, "Central Asia: Emerging Military-Strategic Issues," in Jed C. Snyder (ed.), *After Empire: The Emerging Geopolitics of Central Asia*, NDU Press, Washington, DC, 1995.

Shermatova, Sanobar, "Caspian Faces Threat of Militarization," *Moskovskiye Novosti*, April 19–26, 1998.

Smith, Dianne L., "Central Asia: A New Great Game?" *Asian Affairs*, Vol. 23, Fall 1996, pp. 147–175.

Smith, M. A., *Russia and the Near Abroad*, The Conflict Studies Research Centre, Royal Military Academy, Sandhurst, UK, March 1997.

Sokolsky, Richard, and Tanya Charlick-Paley, "Look Before NATO Leaps Into the Caspian," *Orbis*, Spring 1999, pp. 285–297.

Starr, S. Frederick, "Making Eurasia Stable," *Foreign Affairs*, Vol. 75, No. 1, January/February 1996, pp. 80–92.

_____, "Power Failure: American Policy in the Caspian," *The National Interest*, No. 47, Spring 1997, pp. 20–31.

_____, "U.S. Interests in the Central Asian Republics," testimony before the House Committee on International Relations (Subcommittee on Asia and the Pacific), February 12, 1998, pp. 1–2.

_____, "Central Asian Security: Not a Solo Project," unpublished paper, Nitze School of Advanced International Studies, Johns Hopkins University, Washington, DC, n.d.

Stern, David, "East-West Fault Lines Deepen in Caucasus as NATO Meets," Agence France Presse, April 23, 1999.

"Strategic Policy Toward CIS Published," *Foreign Broadcast Information Service Daily Report*, Central Asia *SOV-95*, September 28, 1995, pp. 14–20.

"Symposium: Caspian Oil," *Middle East Policy*, Vol. 4, No. 4, January 1998, pp. 27–50.

Tellis, Ashley J., Thomas S. Szayna, and James A. Winnefeld, *Anticipating Ethnic Conflict*, RAND, MR-853-A, 1997.

The Military Balance 1997–1998, International Institute for Strategic Studies, Oxford University Press, Oxford, 1998.

Thornhill, John, and Carlotta Gall, "Stability Rooted in Presidential Hands," *Financial Times*, March 3, 1998, pp. 11–12.

Tsepkalo, Valery V., "The Remaking of Eurasia," *Foreign Affairs*, Vol. 77, No. 2, March/April 1998, pp. 107–126.

Turbiville, Graham, "Flashpoints in Central Asia: Sources of Tension and Conflict—Drug and Weapons Trafficking," paper presented at the U.S. Institute of Peace, Washington, DC, May 16, 1997.

_____, *Mafia in Uniform, the Criminalization of the Russian Armed Forces*, Foreign Military Studies Office, July 1995.

_____, "Narcotics Trafficking in Central Asia: A New Colombia," *Military Review*, Vol. LXXII, No. 12, December 1992.

U.S. Department of Energy, *Annual Energy Review 1997*, Energy Information Administration, Washington, DC, 1997.

_____, *International Energy Outlook 1997*, Government Printing Office, Washington, D.C, April 1997.

U.S. Department of State, "Caspian Region Energy Development Report," Washington, DC, April 1997.

Valasek, Tomas, "Arms Buildup or Arms Race?" Center for Defense Information, *Weekly Defense Monitor*, January 28, 1999.

Valencia, Mark, "Energy and Insecurity in Asia," *Survival*, Vol. 3, No. 34, Autumn 1997, pp. 85–106.

Walsh, Richard, "China and the New Geopolitics of Central Asia," *Asian Survey*, Vol. 33, No. 3, March 1993, pp. 272–284.

Washington Post, "Russia Challenged to Disclose Status of BW," February 16, 1998.

Wheatcroft, Stephen G., "Revisiting the Crisis Zones of Euro-Asia, Part Two: The Crisis Zones in 1997," *Russian and Euro-Asian Bulletin*, April 1997, pp. 1–4.

Wimbush, S. Enders, "Central Asia and the Caucasus: Key Emerging Issues and U.S. Interests," unpublished paper prepared for the RAND Conference on Security Dynamics in Central Asia and the Caucasus, March 1998.

Winrow, Gareth, *Turkey in Post-Soviet Central Asia*, Royal Institute of International Affairs, London, 1995.

Xu, Xiaojie, "The Oil and Gas Linkages Between Central Asia and China," paper prepared for the James A. Baker III Institute for Public Policy, Rice University, April 1998.

Zviagelskaia, Irina, *The Russian Policy Debate on Central Asia*, Royal Institute of International Affairs, London, 1995.

Zviagelskaia, Irina, and Vitalii Naumkin, "The Southern Tier: Non-Traditional Threats, Challenges and Risks for Russia's Security," in Rajan Menon, Yuri Fyodorov, and Ghia Nodia (eds.), *Russia, the Caucasus, and Central Asia: The 21st Century Security Environment*, M. E. Sharpe, Armonk, NY, 1999.